BABY BOOMER TRIVIA BOOK

ROCK 'N' ROLL EDITION

CHALLENGE YOURSELF ON THE GREATEST

DECADES OF ROCK

1960s • 1970s • 1980s

Baby Boomer Trivia (Rock n' Roll Edition)

Challenge Yourself on the Greatest Decades of Rock

Copyright © 2025 by **Backstage Classics**

All rights reserved.

No part of this publication may be reproduced, distributed, or transmitted in any form or by any means, including photocopying, recording, or other electronic or mechanical methods, without the prior written permission of the publisher, except in the case of brief quotations embodied in critical reviews and certain other noncommercial uses permitted by copyright law.

Publisher: Backstage Classics

First Edition: 2025

ISBN: 979-8-9932555-4-5

Printed in the United States of America and/or other countries by Amazon KDP.

Cover design: Tasrif Ahmed

Editorial direction: Backstage Classics

DISCLAIMER

This book is an independent work of entertainment and education created by Backstage Classics. It is not authorized, sponsored, or endorsed by any artist, record label, management company, or other entity mentioned within.

All names of bands, performers, songs, and albums are used for historical reference, identification, and educational purposes only under Fair Use.

While every effort has been made to ensure accuracy, some events and accounts are based on publicly available sources, interviews, and historical records that may vary by publication or date.

This book is intended for fans and collectors of rock history. It does not claim to provide definitive or official versions of any disputes, bans, or controversies.

Fact-Checking & Verification Statement:

All trivia questions, answers, and background notes were verified as of 2025 using multiple trusted references, including artist discographies, official chart histories, industry archives, and reputable publications. Backstage Classics maintains a continuous commitment to accuracy and transparency.

It does not provide official interpretations of artist disputes, controversies, or events.

PUBLISHER'S NOTE

Some band names, lyrics, or song titles may reflect language or attitudes from their original era that could be considered offensive today. These are included for historical and cultural accuracy only and do not represent the views or values of the author or publisher.

Backstage Classics celebrates the legacy, creativity, and cultural impact of rock music and strives to present all material with respect for the artists and fans who shaped its history.

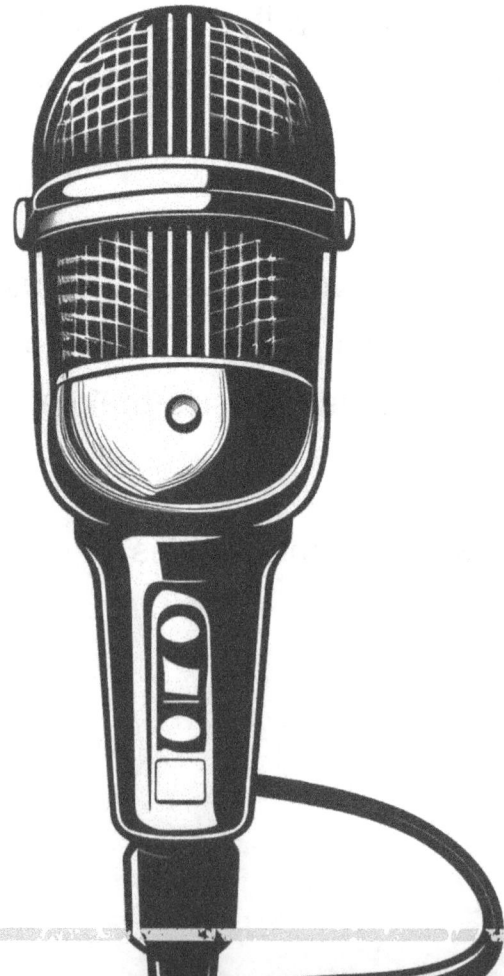

WELCOME TO OUR BABY BOOMER TRIVIA BOOK: ROCK 'N' ROLL EDITION

If you ever flipped a record to Side B just to find the deep cuts, traded bootleg cassettes with friends, or swore you could name a song by the first two notes, **welcome.**

This isn't just a trivia book; it's a time machine built for those who remember when rock ruled every dial, stage, and stereo cabinet. Inside, you'll relive three decades that changed music forever (the 1960s, 1970s, and 1980s) from garage bands and the British Invasion to arena anthems, MTV debuts, and the songs that still bring crowds to their feet.

You'll take on hundreds of questions that test your memory, challenge your expertise, and spark the kind of debates only real fans can have. Expect multiple-choice, true/false, and fill-in-the-blank rounds designed to hit every corner of your rock knowledge.

Between sections, you'll find *Behind the track*, *Did you know?*, and *Remember when…* features packed with stories and trivia worth sharing.

At the end, there is a *Bonus Interlude* with word puzzles and matching games built around the banned, censored, and controversial moments that made headlines.

This book was created by the Backstage Classics team—the same crew behind our YouTube channel, where we celebrate the music, stories, and culture of rock's golden age.

If you want to relive those nights under the lights, catch rare concert footage, or swap memories with other lifelong fans, just search **"Backstage Classics" on YouTube** and join the community that inspired this book.

HOW TO PLAY

Solo Spin: Flip to any part, pick a decade, and see how far your memory goes.

Head-to-Head: Trade questions with a friend; loser buys the next round.

Road Trip Stack: Passenger asks, driver answers, everyone heckles.

Scoring (Suggested):

- Multiple choice: 1 point
- True/False: 1 point
- Fill-in-the-blank (no hints): 2 points
- Tiebreakers: add the song's year, album, or chart peak for +1 bonus point.

Answers are in the back (page 132), numbered for quick reference.

No spoilers while you play! Remember, half the fun is arguing like it's '78.

WHAT YOU'LL EXPERIENCE

Across six themed parts, you'll travel from the rebellion of the '60s to the stadium roar of the '80s through deep-cut stories, concert flashbacks, and the unforgettable chaos that made rock history.

PART I – From Revolutions to Stadiums: The Rise of Rock

British Invasion beginnings, psychedelia, Woodstock, and the birth of hard rock.

PART II – Stadium Power & Arena Glory

The rise of anthems, guitar gods, and the FM sound that filled every arena.

PART III – Behind the Music: Myths, Stories & Deep Cuts

Cult heroes, one-album wonders, and the legends that lived louder offstage.

PART IV – Scandal, Shock & Spectacle

Banned songs, wild tours, and the TV moments that sent parents into orbit.

PART V – The Legacy Lives On

Classic albums, comeback tours, and the lasting influence that still fills arenas today.

PART VI – Concert-Going Nostalgia (For Those Who Were Actually There)

Ticket stubs, tailgate nights, and memories from the pit to the cheap seats.

From Revolutions to Stadiums

The 1960s opened with polite pop and closed with amps powerful enough to shake a stadium. In between, music blew past its old limits and became a way of thinking, dressing, and communicating.

Across the Atlantic, young bands from Liverpool, London, and Manchester hit American radio with an urgency that lit up every garage in the country. Teenagers grabbed bargain guitars, tape machines hissed more than they recorded, and no one chased perfection. They chased electricity.

The songs shifted, too. Lyrics pushed past simple love stories and started questioning the news, the war, and the grown-ups calling the shots. College kids discovered stereo records that filled a room. FM stations broke past the three-minute rule. Festivals exploded from fairgrounds into gatherings built around the music itself.

By the decade's end, everything was louder and heavier. Stacked amps, thunderous drums, and a new definition of "heavy" turned rock into a world with its own heroes, experiments, and unforgettable misfires. If you remember saving for an LP, reading every credit, or hearing a song that made you want to start a band, you're in the right place. The revolution starts here.

ROUND 1

U.S. GARAGE & SURF PIONEERS

Before the full force of the British Invasion hit, American kids were already making noise of their own. In garages, rec rooms, and beach towns, they wired cheap guitars through cracked amplifiers and created a raw, local sound that became the foundation for hard rock and punk. From the surf instrumentals of California to the fuzzed-out riffs of the Midwest, this was the do-it-yourself spirit that kept rock honest.

MULTIPLE CHOICE

1. Which 1963 hit by The Surfaris became one of the defining instrumental anthems of the surf era?

A) *Wipe Out*
B) *Pipeline*
C) *Miserlou*
D) *Surf City*

2. The Kingsmen's 1963 recording of *Louie Louie* gained notoriety because:

A) It was banned for rumored obscene lyrics
B) It was the first stereo single released in the U.S.
C) The band members were all under 16
D) It was recorded live at a high school gym

3. Dick Dale, known as "The King of the Surf Guitar," helped popularize the rapid picking style inspired by which type of music?

A) Spanish flamenco
B) Middle Eastern folk
C) Country western
D) Hawaiian slack-key

4. Which state produced the garage classic *96 Tears* by ? and the Mysterians

A) Texas
B) Illinois
C) Michigan
D) California

5. The 1965 single *Gloria* by Them became a U.S. garage staple after being covered by which Chicago band?

A) The Shadows of Knight
B) The Sonics
C) The Remains
D) The Turtles

6. Which surf-rock duo wrote and performed *Surf City* and later scored hits like *Drag City* and *Dead Man's Curve*?

A) The Ventures
B) The Chantays
C) Jan & Dean
D) The Astronauts

TRUE / FALSE

7. The instrumental hit *Pipeline* was recorded by The Chantays.

8. The Sonics were a Pacific Northwest band whose aggressive sound foreshadowed punk rock.

9. *Wooly Bully* by Sam the Sham & the Pharaohs was first released in 1970.

FILL-IN-THE-BLANK

10. Many early surf-rock recordings featured the distinctive "wet" tone created by _____ reverb amplifiers.

11. Despite the band, The Standells, not being from Boston, their song _____ _____ became an iconic anthem for the city of Boston and teams like the Red Sox.

12. The instrumental *Misirlou*, used decades later in the film *Pulp Fiction*, was originally popularized by guitarist Dick _____.

BEHIND THE TRACK.

"Louie Louie" – The Kingsmen (1963)

Recorded in one take, the track's muffled lyrics triggered a multi-year FBI investigation over claims of obscenity. Agents never found anything offensive, but the rumor only helped the song climb the charts.

ROUND 2

THE BRITISH INVASION

In the early 1960s, a surge of British bands reshaped American radio. Their take on rhythm and blues, melody, and studio craft sparked a musical exchange that still defines classic rock.

MULTIPLE CHOICE

13. The Beatles made their first live U.S. television appearance in February 1964 on which show?

A) *American Bandstand*
B) *Hullabaloo*
C) *Shindig!*
D) *The Ed Sullivan Show*

14. Before forming The Rolling Stones, Mick Jagger and Keith Richards bonded over records by which Chicago bluesman?

A) Muddy Waters
B) Howlin' Wolf
C) B.B. King
D) Elmore James

15. Which 1964 hit by The Animals featured Alan Price's organ riff and became one of the first British Invasion songs to top the U.S. charts?

A) *It's My Life*
B) *We Gotta Get Out of This Place*
C) *Don't Let Me Be Misunderstood*
D) *House of the Rising Sun*

16. The Kinks were barred from touring the United States for four years after a 1965 dispute involving:

A) Work-permit violations
B) On-stage fighting
C) Customs tax issues
D) Stage equipment damage

17. Which London group's anthem *Glad All Over* made them early rivals to the Beatles on both sides of the Atlantic?

A) Manfred Mann
B) The Dave Clark Five
C) The Hollies
D) The Searchers

18. Producer George Martin added a string quartet to which Beatles song in 1965, showing how rock and classical arranging could work together?

A) *Yesterday*
B) *Eleanor Rigby*
C) *Michelle*
D) *Norwegian Wood*

TRUE / FALSE

19. The Rolling Stones took their name from a song title by Muddy Waters.
20. The Beatles' album *Please Please Me* was recorded in a single day at EMI's Abbey Road Studios.
21. Pete Townshend of The Who was still a teenager when he wrote and recorded *My Generation*.

FILL-IN-THE-BLANK

22. The Beatles' 1965 song *Yesterday* was the first rock recording to feature a _____ quartet backing a solo vocal.
23. Before recording *You Really Got Me*, The Kinks created their gritty distortion by slashing an amplifier speaker with a _____ _____.
24. The 1965 single *As Tears Go By* was co-written by Mick Jagger and _____ _____.

BEHIND THE TRACK.

"House of the Rising Sun" – The Animals (1964)

Recorded in one take at London's De Lane Lea Studios, the song's four-minute length pushed radio limits of the time. Its somber Organ line and minor-key mood became a signature of the British Invasion's darker sound.

ROUND 3

PSYCHEDELIA & THE SUMMER OF LOVE

By the mid-1960s, rock music was turning inward. Amplifiers were pushed to new extremes, songs grew longer than radio ever intended, and lyrics shifted toward personal reflection, social consciousness, and surreal imagery. In San Francisco, London, and Los Angeles, bands embraced sitars, feedback, tape experimentation, and studio effects that felt like new dimensions. Rooted in folk and blues but fueled by a rapidly changing culture and the rise of psychedelics, rock transformed into something far more immersive: psychedelic rock.

MULTIPLE CHOICE

25. Which January 14, 1967 festival launched the "Summer of Love" and was a precursor to the Monterey Pop Festival?

A) Altamont Free Concert
B) Human Be-In
C) Isle of Wight Festival
D) Watkins Glen Summer Jam

26. The song *White Rabbit* was written and performed by which San Francisco band fronted by Grace Slick?

A) Big Brother & the Holding Company
B) The Byrds
C) Jefferson Airplane
D) The Mamas & the Papas

27. The Beatles' 1967 album *Sgt. Pepper's Lonely Hearts Club Band* was one of the first to print song lyrics on:

A) the album sleeve
B) a separate lyric booklet
C) the record
D) newspaper advertisements

28. Which British group combined Eastern instruments with pop songwriting on tracks like *Norwegian Wood* and *Within You Without You*?

A) The Kinks
B) The Yardbirds
C) The Beatles
D) The Small Faces

29. Jimi Hendrix famously ended his Monterey Pop performance by:

A) breaking his guitar
B) lighting his guitar on fire
C) throwing his guitar into the crowd
D) smashing the drums

30. Pink Floyd's debut album *The Piper at the Gates of Dawn* was largely shaped by the songwriting and imagination of which founding member?

A) Roger Waters
B) Syd Barrett
C) Richard Wright
D) David Gilmour

TRUE / FALSE

31. The Grateful Dead were originally called The Warlocks before changing their name in 1965.

32. The Byrds' version of *Mr. Tambourine Man* was the first song to feature the sitar as a lead instrument.

33. Janis Joplin performed at both the Monterey Pop Festival and Woodstock.

FILL-IN-THE-BLANK

34. The 1967 single *San Francisco (Be Sure to Wear Some Flowers in Your Hair)* was written by John Phillips and sung by Scott _____.

35. The psychedelic poster art movement of the 1960s was centered in the Haight-Ashbury district of _____ _____, California.

36. The Doors recorded their breakthrough single *Light My Fire* in 1966 at Sunset Studios in _____.

DID YOU KNOW?

The term "psychedelic" predates rock by a decade. Psychiatrist Humphry Osmond used it in 1956 and defined it as "mind manifesting". In rock, some of the first album jackets to use the word arrived in 1966, including The 13th Floor Elevators' The Psychedelic Sounds of the 13th Floor Elevators. That same year, the Deep issued Psychedelic Moods and the Blues Magoos released Psychedelic Lollipop. These 1966 titles mark early commercial use of the word on rock records.

ROUND 4

BREAKTHROUGH ALBUMS OF THE LATE '60S

By the second half of the 1960s, the album became the new canvas for rock music. Artists stopped treating records as bundles of singles and started using sequencing, production, and artwork to make larger statements. Albums like Pet Sounds, Sgt. Pepper's, and Are You Experienced showed that rock could be personal, experimental, and socially aware all at once. These records mirrored the era's change in values and technology, reflecting a generation that wanted music to say more, last longer, and sound unlike anything that came before.

MULTIPLE CHOICE

37. Which 1967 album is often cited as a landmark in studio craft and concept presentation?

A) *Pet Sounds* (The Beach Boys)
B) *Are You Experienced* (The Jimi Hendrix Experience)
C) *Sgt. Pepper's Lonely Hearts Club Band* (The Beatles)
D) *Music from Big Pink* (The Band)

38. Jimi Hendrix's 1967 debut introduced a new guitar vocabulary to rock. Which album was it?

A) *Axis: Bold as Love*
B) *Are You Experienced*
C) *Electric Ladyland*
D) *Smash Hits*

39. Which 1969 release by The Who is widely known as a rock opera?

A) *Tommy*
B) *Who's Next*
C) *Sell Out*
D) *Quadrophenia*

40. Which Led Zeppelin album, released in 1969, includes "Dazed and Confused" and "Good Times Bad Times"?

A) *Led Zeppelin*
B) *Led Zeppelin II*
C) *Led Zeppelin III*
D) *Houses of the Holy*

41. "Gimme Shelter" and "You Can't Always Get What You Want" are key tracks on which 1969 Rolling Stones album?

A) *Beggars Banquet*
B) *Let It Bleed*
C) *Sticky Fingers*
D) *Exile on Main St.*

42. The 1967 album produced under the patronage of Andy Warhol that helped define art-rock minimalism was:

A) *White Light/White Heat* (The Velvet Underground)
B) *The Velvet Underground & Nico*
C) *Loaded* (The Velvet Underground)
D) *Strange Days* (The Doors)

TRUE / FALSE

43. *Pet Sounds* (1966) was released before *Sgt. Pepper's Lonely Hearts Club Band* (1967).

44. Santana's self-titled debut was released after the band's Woodstock appearance in August 1969.

45. *Music from Big Pink* by The Band was recorded in Nashville.

FILL-IN-THE-BLANK

46. The 1969 Beatles album recorded largely at EMI Studios is titled _____ Road.

47. Creedence Clearwater Revival's 1969 album featuring "Fortunate Son" is titled *Willy and the Poor _____*.

48. The 1968 Rolling Stones album that marked a return to roots after psychedelia was _____ *Banquet*.

BEHIND THE TRACK.

"Gimme Shelter" – The Rolling Stones (1969)

Late in the sessions for "Gimme Shelter," producer Jimmy Miller called in Merry Clayton in the middle of the night. She arrived in pajamas, heavily pregnant, to deliver the song's blistering duet. When her voice cracked on a high, emotional note, the intensity was so powerful they kept it on the master, helping turn the track into one of the most iconic and urgent openers in rock history. Tragically, Clayton suffered pregnancy complications afterward that led to a miscarriage, leaving her proud of the performance but unable to listen to the song for years.

ROUND 5

WOODSTOCK & THE COUNTERCULTURE STAGE

In August 1969, hundreds of thousands gathered on a dairy farm in upstate New York for three days of music that ran into a fourth morning. Rain, delays, and shortages could not stop it. The film and the live albums turned several sets into legend and fixed "Woodstock" in rock history.

MULTIPLE CHOICE

49. After permits fell through elsewhere, where did the Woodstock festival actually take place in August 1969?

A) Woodstock, New York
B) Bethel, New York
C) Monticello, New York
D) Wallkill, New York

50. Who closed the festival on Monday morning with an extended set that included a striking version of the national anthem?

A) The Who
B) Crosby, Stills, Nash & Young
C) Jimi Hendrix
D) Jefferson Airplane

51. Which act's performance of "Soul Sacrifice" became a breakout moment captured in the Woodstock documentary film and helped launch their career?

A) Santana
B) Ten Years After
C) Sly and the Family Stone
D) Joe Cocker

52. Which singer wrote the song "Woodstock" but did not attend the festival?

A) Joan Baez
B) Joni Mitchell
C) Grace Slick
D) Janis Joplin

53. Which communal group provided on-site support and "please force" crowd care at the festival?

A) The Diggers
B) The Hog Farm
C) Merry Pranksters
D) Students for a Democratic Society

54. Which act performed immediately before Jimi Hendrix's closing set?

A) Country Joe and the Fish
B) The Band
C) Blood, Sweat & Tears
D) Sha Na Na

TRUE / FALSE

55. The organizers originally planned to hold the festival in Wallkill, New York, but it was moved after local opposition.

56. Crosby, Stills & Nash told the crowd it was only their second time playing in front of people.

57. The Grateful Dead's set is remembered for smooth sound and perfect timing with no technical problems.

FILL-IN-THE-BLANK

58. At Woodstock, there was an onstage announcement that warned the crowds about a batch of "brown _____" that was circulating.

59. Jimi Hendrix's electric version of "The _____ _____ _____" became one of the most discussed moments of Woodstock.

60. Posters and tickets billed Woodstock as "Three Days of _____ and Music."

DID YOU KNOW?

Hendrix did not play to the full weekend crowd. After heavy rain and delays, his set began on Monday morning when many had already left. Estimates suggest fewer than 50,000 remained on the field to see the closing performance, even though total attendance across the weekend reached several hundred thousand.

ROUND 6

EARLY HARD ROCK & PROTO-METAL

By the late 1960s, rock music had grown louder, heavier, and darker. The blues roots were still there, but new amplifiers and recording techniques gave the sound more weight. Distortion, feedback, and power riffs replaced the gentle harmonies of the earlier decade. What began as experimentation in London and Birmingham soon spread around the world, setting the stage for hard rock and heavy metal.

MULTIPLE CHOICE

61. Which band's 1970 self-titled debut is widely regarded as one of the first heavy metal albums?

A) Deep Purple
B) Led Zeppelin
C) Black Sabbath
D) Blue Cheer

62. The Led Zeppelin song *Whole Lotta Love* borrowed from the 1962 track *You Need Love,* written by which Chicago blues songwriter?

A) Willie Dixon
B) Muddy Waters
C) Howlin' Wolf
D) Sonny Boy Williamson

63. Deep Purple's August 1972 live album was recorded over 3 days during concerts in which country?

A) Germany
B) Japan
C) Switzerland
D) Australia

64. Which guitarist for Deep Purple composed the iconic opening riff to *Highway Star* during a 1971 tour rehearsal?

A) Tony Iommi
B) Ritchie Blackmore
C) Jimmy Page
D) Paul Kossoff

65. Blue Cheer's 1968 version of *Summertime Blues* was recorded so loud that it caused problems during:

A) Radio broadcast tests
B) Film
C) Television performances
D) Vinyl mastering

66. Which 1972 Deep Purple single opens with one of the most recognized guitar riffs in rock history?

A) *Highway Star*
B) *Child in Time*
C) *Smoke on the Water*
D) *Woman from Tokyo*

TRUE / FALSE

67. Black Sabbath recorded their debut album in a single day.

68. Led Zeppelin's first album was released before the band ever performed live.

69. Deep Purple began as a psychedelic group before moving toward a heavier sound.

FILL-IN-THE-BLANK

70. The 1971 Uriah Heep song *July* _____ became a cult favorite in Eastern Europe, where fans still gather each year to watch the sunrise on the first day of July.

71. The term "power trio" was commonly used to describe three-piece bands like Cream and The _____ _____ Experience.

72. The 1970 album *Paranoid* featured Black Sabbath's first U.K. Top 10 single, titled _____.

BEHIND THE TRACK.

The song *Paranoid, Black Sabbath* was written and recorded in less than half an hour at Regent Sound Studios in London. The band needed one more track to fill the album, and guitarist Tony Iommi came up with the riff on the spot. Despite the title, the song was not intended to define the album; it simply captured the direct, heavy sound that made Black Sabbath stand apart from their peers.

ROUND 7

FM GOES LONG: ALBUM-ORIENTED ROCK EMERGES

By the early 1970s, FM radio had become the home of rock's next chapter. Stations that once played jazz or classical music began to give more control to disc jockeys who favored longer tracks and full album sides over short singles. Bands responded by creating albums that were meant to be heard in sequence, with songs connected by theme or mood instead of written only for the charts. This approach became known as album-oriented rock. It gave listeners deeper cuts, longer solos, and the sense that rock music had become something to sit and listen to, not just something playing in the background.

MULTIPLE CHOICE

73. The 1971 album that anchored FM playlists with "Baba O'Riley" and "Won't Get Fooled Again" was:

A) *Who Are You*
B) *The Yes Album*
C) *Who's Next*
D) *Quadrophenia*

74. The Allman Brothers Band's *At Fillmore East* (1971) became an FM staple for long improvisations. These performances were recorded in which state?

A) Georgia
B) Florida
C) New York
D) Texas

75. Which 1973 LP is widely cited as a landmark of album-oriented rock for its continuous flow and concept-driven sound?

A) *Close to the Edge* (Yes)
B) *Dark Side of the Moon* (Pink Floyd)
C) *Aqualung* (Jethro Tull)
D) *The Captain and Me* (Doobie Brothers)

76. "Roundabout" became a long-form FM favorite from which 1971 Yes album?

A) *Relayer*
B) *Fragile*
C) *Tales from Topographic Oceans*
D) *Going for the One*

77. Steely Dan's move toward sophisticated, album-centered studio rock was clear on the 1974 LP that featured "Rikki Don't Lose That Number." Which album was it?

A) *Katy Lied*
B) *Countdown to Ecstasy*
C) *Pretzel Logic*
D) *Can't Buy a Thrill*

78. The 1975 album that put Bruce Springsteen on national FM rotation and on both Time and Newsweek covers was:

A) *The Wild, the Innocent & the E Street Shuffle*
B) *Darkness on the Edge of Town*
C) *Nebraska*
D) *Born to Run*

TRUE / FALSE

79. Early AOR stations commonly aired tracks longer than five minutes if they fit the show's flow.

80. Led Zeppelin's 1971 untitled fourth album originally appeared with no band name or title on the cover.

81. Fleetwood Mac's 1975 self-titled album introduced Lindsey Buckingham and Stevie Nicks to the band.

FILL-IN-THE-BLANK

82. The Who's 1971 FM favorite *Baba O'Riley* is often misnamed "_____ _____."

83. Pink Floyd's 1973 hit with a cash-register loop is titled "_____."

84. In the early 1970s, album-oriented stations often aired uninterrupted "_____ blocks" featuring several songs by the same artist.

DID YOU KNOW?

In the late 1960s, free-form FM radio began to tighten its format. What started as open playlists turned into a more organized style that focused on full albums instead of hit singles. DJs still picked deeper cuts, but program directors began shaping consistent "AOR" clocks. That balance of freedom and format helped keep long tracks like "Free Bird," "Won't Get Fooled Again," and "Roundabout" in regular rotation.

ROUND 8

1960S ROCK MILESTONES QUIZ

The 1960s began with three-minute singles and ended with rock albums that filled stadiums. Along the way came artists, songs, and moments that turned popular music into a cultural force. This final round revisits the decade's defining highlights: the breakthroughs, anthems, and firsts that set the stage for everything that followed.

MULTIPLE CHOICE

85. The Beatles' first U.K. No. 1 album, released in 1963, was:

A) *Beatles for Sale*
B) *A Hard Day's Night*
C) *Help!*
D) *Please Please Me*

86. Bob Dylan's decision to "go electric" at which 1965 event shocked folk purists?

A) Monterey Pop Festival
B) Isle of Wight Festival
C) Newport Folk Festival
D) Woodstock

87. Which 1967 single by The Doors opened with Ray Manzarek's organ intro and became a No. 1 hit?

A) *Break On Through*
B) *Light My Fire*
C) *Love Her Madly*
D) *Riders on the Storm*

88. The Rolling Stones earned their first U.S. No. 1 hit in 1965 with:

A) *19th Nervous Breakdown*
B) *Get Off of My Cloud*
C) *(I Can't Get No) Satisfaction*
D) *Paint It Black*

89. Which 1967 debut album introduced Jimi Hendrix's groundbreaking guitar style to a worldwide audience?

A) *Axis: Bold as Love*
B) *Are You Experienced*
C) *Electric Ladyland*
D) *Smash Hits*

90. The Who's 1969 double album that introduced the idea of a "rock opera" was:

A) *Quadrophenia*
B) *Sell Out*
C) *Who's Next*
D) *Tommy*

TRUE / FALSE

91. Jimi Hendrix's U.S. debut at the 1967 Monterey Pop Festival ended with him setting his guitar on fire.

92. The song *Good Vibrations* by The Beach Boys was completed in one recording session.

93. *Music from Big Pink* by The Band (1968) influenced artists including Eric Clapton and George Harrison.

FILL-IN-THE-BLANK

94. The 1969 festival that defined a generation took place about 40 miles southwest of Woodstock, near _____ Lake.

95. Creedence Clearwater Revival's 1969 hit *Fortunate Son* appeared on the album *Willy and the* _____ _____.

96. The Byrds' 1965 recording of *Mr. Tambourine Man* helped launch the folk-_____ movement.

REMEMBER WHEN...

The sound of rock was everywhere. By the end of the 1960s, record stores had full walls of LPs, not singles. Every dorm, car, and basement stereo seemed to hum with needle crackle and guitar feedback. Bands weren't just chasing hits anymore; they were building albums meant to be played from start to finish. Major labels rushed to sign new acts, and radio DJs built entire nights around one side of vinyl. If you can still picture flipping the record, watching the label spin, and letting the next track surprise you, you remember what the end of that decade felt like.

Stadium Power & Arena Glory

By the mid-1970s, rock had outgrown the clubs and college gyms. The sound got louder, the stages got bigger, and the crowds came by the tens of thousands. What started as a rebellion had become a ritual. Denim jackets, tour shirts, and the glow of lighters in the dark became part of the experience.

Every summer brought another road show. Trucks hauled tons of gear from city to city, and crews built stages that could hold walls of speakers. The songs had to reach the cheap seats, so bands wrote anthems built for echo, with power chords, crowd-ready choruses, and hooks that filled stadiums before the first verse ended.

FM radio carried those songs across every highway and backyard. You heard them from factory floors, car stereos, and open windows on a Friday night. The needle dropped on Boston, Styx, Queen, and Journey, and it felt like a call to arms for anyone who still believed in the guitar solo.

Then came the 1980s. The lights got brighter, the hair higher, and the show became as important as the song. MTV brought rock into living rooms and turned stage heroes into household names.

ROUND 9

ARENA ROCK ANTHEMS & SING-ALONG CHORUSES

By the 1970s, rock concerts felt less like shows and more like gatherings. Bands wrote songs built to fill stadiums, with choruses meant to bounce off the rafters and reach the last row. This was the era of anthems, when thousands of voices blended with the ones on stage and the crowd became part of the music itself.

MULTIPLE CHOICE

97. Which 1977 Queen hit became a global sports anthem and a defining sing-along chorus?

A) *Killer Queen*
B) *Somebody to Love*
C) *We Will Rock You*
D) *Radio Ga Ga*

98. Journey's *Don't Stop Believin'* opens with a piano riff played by which member of the band?

A) Neal Schon
B) Jonathan Cain
C) Gregg Rolie
D) Steve Perry

99. Boston's self-titled 1976 debut became one of the best-selling rock albums in history. Which song opened the record?

A) *More Than a Feeling*
B) *Peace of Mind*
C) *Rock and Roll Band*
D) *Foreplay/Long Time*

100. Foreigner's 1977 anthem *Cold as Ice* became a radio and concert favorite. The song appeared on which album?

A) *Double Vision*
B) *Foreigner*
C) *Head Games*
D) *4*

101. Cheap Trick's *I Want You to Want Me* became an arena favorite after being recorded live in which country?

A) United States
B) Australia
C) England
D) Japan

102. The 1976 Kansas single that became a fan sing-along and end-of-show tradition was:

A) *Dust in the Wind*
B) *Point of Know Return*
C) *Carry On Wayward Son*
D) *Song for America*

TRUE / FALSE

103. The crowd-stomping rhythm of *We Will Rock You* was inspired by Queen's attempt to get audiences more involved during live shows.

104. Foreigner's *Juke Box Hero* was inspired by a real fan who waited outside a concert venue hoping to meet the band.

105. *Don't Fear the Reaper* by Blue Öyster Cult became a 1976 FM favorite and live staple later known for its cowbell-heavy rhythm, thanks to a Saturday Night Live sketch.

FILL-IN-THE-BLANK

106. The song *Carry On Wayward Son* by Kansas was written by guitarist Kerry _____.

107. *We Are the Champions* was often performed back-to-back with _____ _____ _____ _____ in concerts.

108. Boston's 1976 debut album was produced and engineered by guitarist Tom _____.

BEHIND THE TRACK.

"More Than a Feeling" – Boston (1976)

Tom Scholz spent five years recording *More Than a Feeling* in his basement studio, layering guitars and vocal tracks one by one. Its mix of precision and emotion became the blueprint for countless anthems that followed.

ROUND 10

CLASSIC ROCK RADIO KINGS

These were the records that never left rotation, the guitar tones and voices that became shorthand for the era itself. Whether it was The Eagles in Los Angeles, Seger in the Midwest, or Skynyrd in the South, their songs played from every dashboard and bar jukebox. They were setting the standard for what rock would sound like for generations.

MULTIPLE CHOICE

109. Which Eagles song from 1976 opens with a 12-string guitar and became one of the most-played tracks in FM radio history?

A) *Take It Easy*
B) *Hotel California*
C) *Already Gone*
D) *Peaceful Easy Feeling*

110. Bob Seger's *Night Moves* was inspired by his teenage years in which U.S. state?

A) Indiana
B) Michigan
C) Illinois
D) Ohio

111. Lynyrd Skynyrd's *Sweet Home Alabama* was written as a response to which artist's earlier songs about the American South?

A) Bob Dylan
B) John Fogerty
C) Bruce Springsteen
D) Neil Young

112. The 1973 Allman Brothers Band song *Ramblin' Man* helped bring Southern rock to national radio. Which guitarist sang lead vocals on it?

A) Duane Allman
B) Gregg Allman
C) Warren Haynes
D) Dickey Betts

113. Tom Petty and the Heartbreakers' *Refugee* appeared on which 1979 album?

A) *Damn the Torpedoes*
B) *Hard Promises*
C) *Southern Accents*
D) *You're Gonna Get It!*

114. Which Billy Joel song from 1977 became a classic rock mainstay and remains one of his most performed live tracks?

A) *Movin' Out (Anthony's Song)*
B) *Scenes from an Italian Restaurant*
C) *The Stranger*
D) *Only the Good Die Young*

TRUE / FALSE

115. Lynyrd Skynyrd's *Free Bird* was originally written as a tribute to Allman Brothers guitarist Duane Allman.

116. Bob Seger's *Turn the Page* was first released as a live recording rather than a studio single.

117. *Hotel California* was recorded using three separate guitar parts layered together to achieve its signature outro solo.

FILL-IN-THE-BLANK

118. The 1977 Fleetwood Mac hit *Go Your Own Way* was written by guitarist _____ _____.

119. The 1977 Steve Miller Band single *Jet* _____ became one of the most-played songs on classic rock radio and a concert favorite.

120. The Eagles' longtime manager and producer was Bill _____, who helped shape the sound of *Hotel California*.

DID YOU KNOW?

When *American Pie* by Don McLean was released in 1971, it ran over eight minutes long. Instead of cutting it down, DJs at WABC and WNEW in New York played the full version on air and listeners stayed tuned through the entire thing. That moment helped convince FM programmers that long songs could hold attention, paving the way for airplay of *Layla*, *Free Bird*, and *Hotel California* in their full form.

ROUND 11

POWER BALLADS & BIG HOOKS

By the end of the 1970s, rock found a new balance between volume and melody. Bands discovered that a single slow song could fill arenas just as easily as the loudest guitar riff. Power ballads and big-hook anthems ruled the charts, carried by strong vocals, layered production, and emotional intensity that made fans sing every word.

MULTIPLE CHOICE

121. Which Journey song from 1981 became one of the best-selling digital tracks of the 20th century and a staple of arena encores?

A) *Faithfully*
B) *Don't Stop Believin'*
C) *Separate Ways*
D) *Open Arms*

122. REO Speedwagon's *Keep On Loving You* reached number one on the Billboard Hot 100 in what year?

A) 1979
B) 1980
C) 1981
D) 1982

123. Which Foreigner single became their first number-one hit on both U.S. and U.K. charts in 1984?

A) *Urgent*
B) *Cold as Ice*
C) *I Want to Know What Love Is*
D) *Waiting for a Girl Like You*

124. The 1983 Def Leppard song *Photograph* marked a shift toward a more polished arena sound. Which producer helped craft its layered style?

A) Mutt Lange
B) Bob Rock
C) Roy Thomas Baker
D) Tom Werman

125. Which Scorpions ballad from 1984 became one of the first heavy-metal songs to receive extensive MTV airplay?

A) *Still Loving You*
B) *No One Like You*
C) *Holiday*
D) *Always Somewhere*

126. Heart's *Alone* became a U.S. chart-topper in 1987 and featured which sisters as co-leaders of the band?

A) Nancy and Ann Wilson
B) Robin and Debra Wilson
C) Kim and Kelly Deal
D) Susanna and Kathy Hoffs

TRUE / FALSE

127. *Every Rose Has Its Thorn* by Poison was written after the band's lead singer heard another man's voice in the background while on the phone with his girlfriend.

128. Def Leppard's *Photograph* was banned by some British TV stations for its suggestive lyrics.

129. Foreigner recorded *I Want to Know What Love Is* with a gospel choir from New Jersey.

FILL-IN-THE-BLANK

130. The 1982 Survivor hit *Eye _____ _____ _____* became the theme for *Rocky III* and topped charts worldwide.

131. Bon Jovi's 1986 album *Slippery _____ _____* produced multiple arena anthems, including *Livin' on a Prayer*, "You Give Love a Bad Name", and "Wanted Dead or Alive".

132. *Love Bites* became Def Leppard's first number-one single on the Billboard Hot 100 in _____.

BEHIND THE TRACK.

"I Want to Know What Love Is" – Foreigner (1984)

The recording featured the New Jersey Mass Choir, gospel singer Jennifer Holliday, and the Thompson Twins providing backing vocals. It became Foreigner's first number-one single, topping charts in more than a dozen countries and remaining one of the most recognized power ballads of the 1980s.

ROUND 12

U.S. VS. BRITISH ROCK RIVALRIES

Throughout the 1970s and 1980s, rock music was defined by a friendly but fierce competition between American and British acts. British bands often dominated the global charts first, while U.S. artists fired back with stadium tours, radio staples, and massive record sales. This rivalry shaped everything from sound to image, giving rise to some of the most enduring names in rock.

MULTIPLE CHOICE

133. Which British band's success in the U.S. during the 1980s helped spark a second "British Invasion"?

A) The Who
B) Queen
C) The Police
D) Pink Floyd

134. Bruce Springsteen's 1984 album *Born in the U.S.A.* sold over 17 million copies worldwide, directly competing with which British superstar's *Let's Dance* that same year?

A) Elton John
B) Phil Collins
C) David Bowie
D) Sting

135. Van Halen's *Jump* topped U.S. charts in 1984, the same year which British band released *1984 (For the Love of Big Brother)* inspired by George Orwell's novel?

A) Eurythmics
B) Def Leppard
C) Dire Straits
D) The Police

136. Dire Straits' *Money for Nothing* became a worldwide hit partly due to early MTV airplay. The song includes a cameo vocal appearance by which American musician?

A) Billy Joel
B) Huey Lewis
C) Bob Dylan
D) Sting

137. Which American band was often compared to Queen for its mix of hard rock and theatrical stage shows?

A) Van Halen
B) Aerosmith
C) Journey
D) Styx

138. In 1985, U.S. artists recorded *We Are the World* as a charity single. It was partly inspired by which British-led project released earlier that same year?

A) *Do They Know It's Christmas?*
B) *Give Peace a Chance*
C) *Feed the World*
D) *Love Song for Africa*

TRUE / FALSE

139. American band Blue Öyster Cult was one of the first to combine hard rock and science fiction themes in both lyrics and stage design.

140. The British group Thin Lizzy was formed by members of Free, Mott the Hoople, and King Crimson.

141. REO Speedwagon's *Hi Infidelity* sold more copies in the United States than any Def Leppard album during the 1980s.

FILL-IN-THE-BLANK

142. The 1976 Electric Light Orchestra hit *Livin' Thing* blended classical arrangements with rock hooks, a hallmark of the _____ _____ sound.

143. The 1983 U.S. Festival in California was organized by Apple co-founder _____ Wozniak.

144. The 1977 Thin Lizzy single *The Boys Are* _____ _____ _____ became one of the band's signature songs in both the U.K. and the U.S.

REMEMBER WHEN...

Millions of fans on both sides of the Atlantic tuned in for Live Aid in July of 1985. Wembley Stadium in London and JFK Stadium in Philadelphia hosted the daylong concert to raise money for famine relief in Ethiopia. British and American acts shared the spotlight, with Queen's set in London still remembered as one of the greatest live performances ever. Led Zeppelin reunited in Philadelphia with Phil Collins and Tony Thompson taking over on drums for the late John Bonham. Broadcast across more than 150 countries, the event reached nearly two billion viewers and proved that rock music could unite the world for a cause.

ROUND 13

MTV ROCK BREAKOUTS

When MTV launched on August 1, 1981, rock bands suddenly needed more than sound. They needed image, attitude, and video appeal. The new channel turned rising acts into global names and gave rock music a fresh visual language. These years marked a second explosion of arena-ready hits, this time powered by the television screen.

MULTIPLE CHOICE

145. What was the first music video broadcast on MTV when the network launched in 1981?

A) *Don't Stand So Close to Me* – The Police
B) *You Better You Bet* – The Who
C) *Jessie's Girl* – Rick Springfield
D) *Video Killed the Radio Star* – The Buggles

146. Which British band's 1983 video for *Union of the Snake* was one of MTV's most expensive productions at the time?

A) Duran Duran
B) The Police
C) Tears for Fears
D) Simple Minds

147. Which American artist became one of MTV's first female rock icons with the 1983 hit *Love Is a Battlefield*?

A) Pat Benatar
B) Joan Jett
C) Heart
D) Stevie Nicks

148. Van Halen's *Jump* music video featured footage of the band performing on a soundstage. It was filmed during which year?

A) 1982
B) 1983
C) 1984
D) 1985

149. Which British rock group used groundbreaking animation in the 1985 video for *Money for Nothing*?

A) Genesis
B) Dire Straits
C) The Police
D) Yes

150. Which American band's video for *You Might Think* won the first-ever MTV Video of the Year award in 1984?

A) The Cars
B) ZZ Top
C) Huey Lewis and the News
D) Journey

TRUE / FALSE

151. MTV originally broadcast only in parts of New Jersey before expanding nationwide through cable networks.

152. MTV stopped airing all rock videos in 1985 after switching to pop-only programming.

153. ZZ Top's music videos for *Sharp Dressed Man* and *Legs* helped the band reach a younger audience during the 1980s.

FILL-IN-THE-BLANK

154. The Police filmed the 1983 video for *Every Breath You Take* entirely in _____ _____ _____.

155. The MTV Video Music Awards (VMAs) began in _____.

156. The 1984 *Jump* video featured guitarist Eddie _____ _____ using his famous red, white, and black striped guitar.

REMEMBER WHEN...

When MTV first aired in 1981, most cable systems didn't even carry it yet. Fans who could tune in passed word to friends, and groups would gather just to watch new videos together. In fact, many of the VJs and staff had to go to New Jersey to watch the channel because it was not yet available on New York City's cable provider. Viewers saw Pat Benatar, The Cars, and Van Halen on repeat because MTV had so few clips to rotate. By 1983, the lineup had exploded, and a good video could make a band a household name overnight.

ROUND 14

GUITAR HEROES & SOLO LEGENDS

In the 1970s and 1980s, the guitar wasn't just part of the band… It was the headline act. Players pushed sound and style in every direction, from high-speed solos to slow bends that could stop a crowd cold. New gear, louder amps, and emerging studio effects gave each player a voice of their own, turning the instrument into the defining symbol of rock itself.

MULTIPLE CHOICE

157. Which guitarist developed the "tapping" technique that became a defining sound of 1980s rock?

A) Randy Rhoads
B) Eddie Van Halen
C) Steve Vai
D) Yngwie Malmsteen

158. Jeff Beck's 1975 album *Blow by Blow* was groundbreaking for mixing guitar rock with what genre?

A) Folk
B) Disco
C) Country
D) Jazz fusion

159. Carlos Santana gained international fame after performing at which 1969 festival?

A) Monterey Pop
B) Woodstock
C) Isle of Wight
D) Atlanta International Pop Festival

160. Which British guitarist replaced Ritchie Blackmore in Deep Purple during the mid-1970s?

A) Gary Moore
B) Steve Morse
C) Tommy Bolin
D) Robin Trower

161. The 1983 album *Texas Flood* launched the career of which American blues-rock guitarist?

A) Stevie Ray Vaughan
B) Billy Gibbons
C) Joe Walsh
D) Gary Moore

162. Which Pink Floyd guitarist and vocalist became known for his soaring solos on tracks like *Comfortably Numb*?

A) Jimmy Page
B) David Gilmour
C) Andy Summers
D) Syd Barrett

TRUE / FALSE

163. Angus Young of AC/DC often played a Gibson Les Paul during live shows.

164. Eric Clapton was the first British artist to earn three separate inductions into the Rock and Roll Hall of Fame

165. Steve Vai and Joe Satriani were both students of the same guitar teacher before becoming solo stars.

FILL-IN-THE-BLANK

166. Eddie Van Halen's custom red, white, and black guitar was famously nicknamed the "_____."

167. Joe Satriani's 1987 instrumental *Surfing with the* _____ *Mind* became one of the most successful guitar albums of the decade.

168. Randy Rhoads recorded *Crazy Train* with Ozzy Osbourne in 1980, featuring one of rock's most recognizable opening riffs. The song appeared on the album _____ _____ _____.

BEHIND THE TRACK.

"Texas Flood" – Stevie Ray Vaughan (1983)

The entire *Texas Flood* album, including the title track, was recorded in a very short, three-day (essentially live) session at Jackson Browne's personal studio in Los Angeles during Thanksgiving weekend of 1982.

ROUND 15

FRONTMEN WHO RULED THE STAGE

In every great rock band, the frontman set the tone. They connected the crowd to the music, controlled the pace of the show, and turned concerts into events people still talk about. Whether through power, charisma, or sheer confidence, these singers defined what it meant to lead a band on stage.

MULTIPLE CHOICE

169. Which Scottish singer became known for his theatrical style and commanding stage presence as the frontman of Ultravox?

A) Midge Ure
B) Simon Le Bon
C) Marc Almond
D) Jim Kerr

170. David Coverdale first gained attention as Deep Purple's lead vocalist before forming which successful band in 1978?

A) Asia
B) Whitesnake
C) Bad English
D) Rainbow

171. Which American frontman was known for leading theatrical shock-rock performances featuring guillotines, snakes, and fake blood?

A) Rob Halford
B) Ozzy Osbourne
C) Alice Cooper
D) Blackie Lawless

172. Phil Lynott, bassist and singer for Thin Lizzy, was known for writing and performing which 1976 live favorite?

A) *Killer On The Loose*
B) *Emerald*
C) *The Boys Are Back in Town*
D) *Cowboy Song*

173. Which British singer led the band UFO and was praised for his powerful, blues-based vocal delivery during the 1970s?

A) Phil Mogg
B) Paul Rodgers
C) Joe Elliott
D) John Waite

174. Billy Idol's 1982 solo debut helped define the look and attitude of early MTV-era rock. Which single was his first U.S. Top 40 hit?

A) *Rebel Yell*
B) *Hot in the City*
C) *Eyes Without a Face*
D) *Dancing with Myself*

TRUE / FALSE

175. Peter Gabriel left Genesis in 1975, where he had become known for wearing elaborate costumes and theatrical makeup during live performances.
176. Lou Gramm of Foreigner started his career as a drummer before becoming a lead singer.
177. Bon Scott of AC/DC once worked as a postal clerk before joining the band in 1974.

FILL-IN-THE-BLANK

178. The 1979 live album *Strangers* _____ _____ _____ captured UFO's dynamic performances with Phil Mogg on vocals.
179. The 1981 hit *Urgent* featured powerful vocals by Foreigner's lead singer Lou _____.
180. Phil Lynott's final studio album with Thin Lizzy was _____ _____ _____ in 1983.

BEHIND THE TRACK.

"White Wedding" – Billy Idol (1982)

Filmed in stark black and white, the video for *White Wedding* became an early MTV landmark and helped define Billy Idol's rebellious image. The song's mix of punk energy and pop precision made Idol one of the first British artists to cross over into mainstream American rock through television exposure.

ROUND 16

WOMEN WHO ROCKED THE AIRWAVES

By the late 1970s, women in rock were no longer the exception. They were headliners, hitmakers, and bandleaders whose songs ruled FM playlists and MTV rotations. Their voices carried power and range, and their presence reshaped how audiences saw rock performance.

MULTIPLE CHOICE

181. Which American singer became the first female artist to write, produce, and perform a Billboard Hot 100 number-one single entirely by herself?

A) Madonna
B) Janet Jackson
C) Joan Jett
D) Debbie Gibson

182. The 1983 single *Total Eclipse of the Heart* became a worldwide hit for which Welsh singer?

A) Bonnie Tyler
B) Kim Wilde
C) Annie Lennox
D) Pat Benatar

183. Debbie Harry was the frontwoman of which band that fused punk, pop, and new wave influences in the late 1970s?

A) Missing Persons
B) The Pretenders
C) Blondie
D) Siouxsie and the Banshees

184. Which Canadian artist reached the Top 10 in 1989 with the song *Black Velvet*, inspired by Elvis Presley?

A) Alannah Myles
B) Sass Jordan
C) Robin Beck
D) Lee Aaron

185. The 1980 album *Crimes of Passion* produced four hit singles for which powerhouse vocalist?

A) Ann Wilson
B) Pat Benatar
C) Kim Carnes
D) Nancy Wilson

186. Which English duo, fronted by Annie Lennox, scored multiple hits in the 1980s including *Sweet Dreams (Are Made of This)*?

A) Roxette
B) Berlin
C) Eurythmics
D) The Motels

TRUE / FALSE

187. Joan Jett's *I Love Rock 'n' Roll* was originally recorded by a British band before she turned it into a U.S. hit.

188. Pat Benatar trained as a classical soprano before becoming a rock singer.

189. Debbie Harry started Blondie as a solo act before hiring a backing band.

FILL-IN-THE-BLANK

190. The 1984 single *The Warrior* featured lead vocals by Patty _____, frontwoman of Scandal.

191. *Love Is a Battlefield* earned Pat Benatar a Grammy Award for Best Female Rock _____ _____.

192. Stevie Nicks's 1981 debut solo album was titled *Bella* _____.

BEHIND THE TRACK.

"Sweet Dreams (Are Made of This)" – Eurythmics (1983)

The Eurythmics recorded *Sweet Dreams (Are Made of This)* using equipment they bought with a low budget after being dropped by their previous label. They built the song around a Roland synthesizer riff programmed by Dave Stewart, with Annie Lennox layering her vocals in a single night.

Behind the Music: Myths, Stories & Deep Cuts

Not every great band filled arenas. Some played to half-empty clubs, traded tapes through fanzines, or lived on late-night FM radio shows that only the most dedicated listeners could find. The 1970s underground thrived in these corners. These were the places where sound mattered more than sales and where word-of-mouth built legends one record at a time.

Collectors chased imports, white-label pressings, and promo copies passed from DJ to DJ. A new kind of listener emerged: the fan who memorized liner notes, followed producer credits, and built their own education from used record bins. The same decade that gave us platinum albums also gave us cult heroes and artists who pushed ideas further than the charts ever allowed.

By the 1980s, some of these names resurfaced on reissues, documentaries, or collector forums. Others stayed lost, remembered only by those who taped songs off the radio and kept the labels from fading. This section is for the ones who know that rock history doesn't just live in the hits. It lives in the grooves that only a few have heard.

ROUND 17

LOST BANDS OF THE '70S

The 1970s produced hundreds of bands that came close to breaking through but never reached household-name status. Some faded after one album. Others were undone by label issues, lineup changes, or bad timing. Decades later, collectors still hunt for these records.

MULTIPLE CHOICE

193. The British band Free is best known for *All Right Now*, but which short-lived follow-up group featured two of its members and dissolved after one album?

A) Bad Company
B) Peace
C) Kossoff, Kirke, Tetsu & Rabbit
D) Trapeze

194. Which American band, fronted by Lowell George, blended rock, funk, and country on cult albums like *Sailin' Shoes* and *Dixie Chicken*?

A) Little Feat
B) Orleans
C) Pure Prairie League
D) The Doobie Brothers

195. The power trio Trapeze featured which future Deep Purple and Black Sabbath member on bass and vocals?

A) Glenn Hughes
B) Roger Glover
C) Geezer Butler
D) Jack Bruce

196. Starz, often considered a missing link between glam and hard rock, was originally managed by which KISS associate?

A) Bill Aucoin
B) Neil Bogart
C) Paul Stanley
D) Eddie Kramer

197. The British group Be-Bop Deluxe, led by guitarist Bill Nelson, mixed art-rock style with guitar virtuosity. Which 1976 album featured the single *Ships in the Night*?

A) *Futurama*
B) *Drastic Plastic*
C) *Modern Music*
D) *Sunburst Finish*

198. The San Francisco band Clover, which recorded several overlooked 1970s albums, is best known today for launching which future star's career?

A) Eddie Money
B) Huey Lewis
C) Tom Petty
D) Jackson Browne

TRUE / FALSE

199. After Ian Hunter left in 1974, the remaining members of Mott the Hoople continued as Mott, while guitarist Mick Ralphs had already departed in 1973 to form Bad Company.

200. American band Detective was signed to Led Zeppelin's Swan Song label but never released a studio album.

201. The British band Argent took its name from keyboardist Rod Argent, formerly of The Zombies.

FILL-IN-THE-BLANK

202. The band Armageddon, featuring former Yardbirds vocalist Keith _____, released only one album in 1975 before disbanding.

203. American progressive outfit Pavlov's _____ built a cult following with their blend of horn rock and jazz influences.

204. The short-lived British group Widowmaker featured Ariel Bender from Mott the Hoople and Huw _____-_____ from Hawkwind.

DID YOU KNOW?

Many "lost" bands of the 1970s have been rediscovered through digital reissues and vinyl collectors. Labels such as Repertoire, Esoteric, and Wounded Bird have brought back albums once available only as imports or bootlegs. Online forums and record fairs continue to uncover forgotten masters, proving that the decade's depth went far beyond the hits.

ROUND 18

ONE-ALBUM WONDERS

Some bands left behind only one studio album that captured a moment, earned a few devoted fans, and then disappeared. Many of these releases never reached radio but became staples for collectors and late-night DJs who prized originality over fame. These are the true one-album wonders of the rock underground.

MULTIPLE CHOICE

205. Which British hard-rock group released their only album *Armageddon* in 1975, featuring former members of The Yardbirds and Renaissance?

A) Tucky Buzzard
B) Stray Dog
C) Armageddon
D) Widowmaker

206. The 1971 British band *Titus Groan* released their only album blending progressive and jazz-rock styles. The group took its name from a novel by which author?

A) Mervyn Peake
B) J.R.R. Tolkien
C) Michael Moorcock
D) Aldous Huxley

207. Captain Beyond, formed by former members of Deep Purple and Iron Butterfly, released their debut album in 1972. How many original studio albums followed with the same lineup?

A) Three
B) One
C) Two
D) None

208. The British blues-rock outfit Leaf Hound became a collector favorite for their 1971 album *Growers of* _____.

A) Dreams
B) Mushrooms
C) Thorns
D) Giants

209. The British hard-rock band *Hard Stuff* featured John Cann and Paul Hammond, both formerly of Atomic Rooster. Their only 1972 album released under the name *Bulletproof* came out on which major label?

A) Harvest
B) Island
C) A&M
D) Purple Records

210. The short-lived band Jerusalem released a single self-titled album in 1972 produced by which Deep Purple member?

A) Ian Gillan
B) Glenn Hughes
C) Nick Simper
D) John Gustafson

TRUE / FALSE

211. The group T2's 1970 album *It'll All Work Out in Boomland* has since become one of the most valuable U.K. progressive-rock records on vinyl.

212. The band Ancient Grease from Wales released two studio albums before disbanding.

213. The heavy-rock band Ashkan featured future Fleetwood Mac guitarist Bob Weston on their sole 1969 LP.

FILL-IN-THE-BLANK

214. The 1970 self-titled album by the band Cressida became a cornerstone of the Vertigo "swirl" label's early _____-rock catalog.

215. The 1971 album *Affinity* featured vocalist Linda _____, who later sang with jazz and soul groups.

216. The 1970 album *Indian _____* by the group of the same name blended psychedelic and early hard-rock elements before the band disappeared.

DID YOU KNOW?

Many one-album acts gained recognition decades later thanks to European reissue labels. Collectors in Japan and Germany began rediscovering obscure titles, driving prices of original pressings into the thousands. These albums, once obscure studio experiments, are now widely regarded as essential and influential parts of underground rock, prog rock, and early heavy metal history, thanks to the reissue market.

ROUND 19

UNDERRATED GUITAR GODS

Beyond the headliners and guitar heroes who filled arenas, a quieter league of players shaped the sound of rock from the shadows. They rarely appeared on magazine covers, but they left an impression on generations of musicians who listened closely. These are the guitarists known best by those who read liner notes front to back.

MULTIPLE CHOICE

217. Mick Ronson, best known for his work with David Bowie, released a solo debut in 1974 titled *Slaughter on _____ Avenue.*

A) 5th
B) 8th
C) 10th
D) 12th

218. Robin Trower, a former member of Procol Harum, became known for his soulful tone on the 1974 album *Bridge of _____.*

A) Dreams
B) Sighs
C) Fire
D) Light

219. Guitarist Rory Gallagher earned a devoted following through relentless touring and live albums but never had a U.S. Top 40 hit. He was born in which country?

A) Scotland
B) Ireland
C) Wales
D) England

220. The late Paul Kossoff, known for his emotional vibrato style, was a founding member of which British blues-rock band?

A) Free
B) Savoy Brown
C) Taste
D) Trapeze

221. Which American guitarist was known for blending jazz and rock on albums such as *Blow by Blow* and *Wired* during the mid-1970s?

A) Al Di Meola
B) Steve Howe
C) Jeff Beck
D) Tommy Bolin

222. Tommy Bolin, who briefly played with Deep Purple, released a 1975 solo album titled *Teaser* before his death at age _____.

A) 25
B) 27
C) 29
D) 31

TRUE / FALSE

223. Rory Gallagher famously turned down an offer to join The Rolling Stones in the early 1970s.

224. Robin Trower often performed using a Gibson Les Paul throughout his solo career.

225. Gary Moore's early career included a stint with the Irish band Skid Row before joining Thin Lizzy.

FILL-IN-THE-BLANK

226. Paul Kossoff released a 1973 solo album titled *Back* _____ _____ and later formed a band with the same name.

227. Guitarist Gary Moore's 1978 album *Back on the Streets* included the hit single "Parisienne _____," featuring vocals by Phil Lynott of Thin Lizzy.

228. Jeff Beck's instrumental *Cause We've Ended as Lovers* was written by Stevie _____.

BEHIND THE TRACK.

"Bullfrog Blues" – Rory Gallagher (1972)

Captured live during his 1972 European tour, "Bullfrog Blues" showcased Rory Gallagher's raw, unpolished blues-rock energy using his famous, battle-scarred 1961 Fender Stratocaster. The performance was recorded directly from the stage with a mobile unit, providing a stripped-down, natural tone that helped shape the sound of '70s hard rock.

ROUND 20

OVERLOOKED PROG & ART-ROCK HEROES

In the shadows of arena tours and radio countdowns, another branch of rock was quietly rewriting the rules. These musicians cared less about hooks and more about ideas and lyrics that read like short stories. College stations and import bins kept their music alive, passed hand to hand by listeners who wanted something beyond the singles chart.

MULTIPLE CHOICE

229. Which band released the largely instrumental concept album *The Snow Goose* in 1975?

A) Nektar
B) Camel
C) Gryphon
D) Renaissance

230. The 1971 album *Pawn Hearts* (featuring the side-long "A Plague of Lighthouse Keepers") is by which group?

A) Van der Graaf Generator
B) Barclay James Harvest
C) Audience
D) Curved Air

231. Known for counterpoint vocals and complex arrangements, which band issued *Octopus* in 1972?

A) Caravan
B) The Enid
C) Gentle Giant
D) Egg

232. The 1973 concept album *Remember the Future* reached the U.S. Top 20 for which act?

A) Be-Bop Deluxe
B) Nektar
C) Strawbs
D) Colosseum II

233. Which singer is associated with Renaissance's symphonic-rock era, including the 1978 single "Northern Lights"?

A) Sonja Kristina
B) Annie Haslam
C) Sandy Denny
D) Judy Dyble

234. Which art-rock group brought electric violin to the frontline on tracks like "Back Street Luv" (1971)?

A) Curved Air
B) Barclay James Harvest
C) Audience
D) Greenslade

TRUE / FALSE

235. Van der Graaf Generator released key early-'70s albums on Charisma Records.

236. *The Snow Goose* was originally issued with lead vocals on all tracks.

237. Gentle Giant members often switched instruments on stage and in the studio, reflecting formal musical training.

FILL-IN-THE-BLANK

238. The British band Barclay James _____ blended orchestral textures with melodic rock during the 1970s.

239. Italian prog pioneers Premiata _____ _____ are often abbreviated as PFM.

240. The Enid's 1976 debut *In the Region of the Summer Stars* was largely _____.

REMEMBER WHEN...

You could tune in after midnight and catch something completely new — a band you'd never heard of, playing live on BBC Radio with no crowd and no polish. DJs like John Peel gave airtime to groups that couldn't get past the major labels, and those late-night sessions turned into prized cassette recordings traded among fans.

ROUND 21

REMEMBERING FM FAVORITES

When FM radio was king, every drive had a soundtrack. The airwaves carried the voices and melodies that defined the '70s and early '80s — songs that played in diners, garages, and through open car windows on summer nights. Long before digital playlists, these tracks connected people across cities and generations. Some became anthems, others quiet companions, but all of them remind listeners of a time when turning the dial was part of the ritual.

MULTIPLE CHOICE

241. The Atlanta Rhythm Section reached No. 7 on the Billboard Hot 100 in 1978 with *Imaginary _____*.

A) Woman
B) Lover
C) Friend
D) Girl

242. The 1975 song *Sister Golden Hair* was a No. 1 hit for which American soft-rock trio?

A) Orleans
B) America
C) Firefall
D) Ambrosia

243. The band Pablo Cruise was best known for which 1977 single that became a radio mainstay?

A) Whatcha Gonna Do?
B) Cool Love
C) Love Will Find a Way
D) I Go to Rio

244. The Sanford-Townsend Band had a one-hit wonder with their 1977 single *Smoke from a _____*.

A) Gun
B) Candle
C) Fire
D) Match

245. The song *So Into You* was released in 1977 by which Southern rock band known for blending funk and pop influences?

A) Wet Willie
B) Atlanta Rhythm Section
C) The Outlaws
D) Starbuck

246. Which group's 1978 single *Dance With Me* featured acoustic guitar and harmonies that made it a soft-rock FM staple?

A) Orleans
B) Player
C) Ambrosia
D) Firefall

TRUE / FALSE

247. Player's *Baby Come Back* reached No. 1 on the Billboard Hot 100 in 1976.

248. The band Ambrosia began as a progressive-rock act before moving toward soft-rock and pop in the late 1970s.

249. Firefall's *You Are the Woman* was released in 1982.

FILL-IN-THE-BLANK

250. *Fooled Around and Fell in Love* featured vocals by Mickey _____, later of Jefferson Starship.

251. The 1975 single *Miracles* featured the distinctive vocals of Marty _____, frontman for Jefferson Starship.

252. The 1977 Steve Miller Band hit *Jet Airliner* was written by songwriter _____ _____, whose version first appeared a year earlier.

BEHIND THE TRACK.

"Driver's Seat" – Sniff 'n' the Tears (1978)

Recorded in London on a modest budget, "Driver's Seat" was built around drummer Luigi Salvoni's tight, hypnotic groove and Paul Roberts's atmospheric songwriting. Its steady rhythm and moody tone caught the attention of late-night FM DJs in the U.S., helping the song climb to No. 15 on the Billboard Hot 100 in 1979. Though it just missed the Top 10, "Driver's Seat" became an enduring American radio staple and later resurfaced in films and commercials, securing its status as a cult classic of late-'70s rock.

ROUND 22

CULT METAL & UNDERGROUND SCENES

Before heavy metal filled arenas, it survived in garages, pubs, and clubs where sound traveled through tape trading and late-night radio. The fans were few but loyal, swapping demos and setlists like currency. These bands shaped the next wave of metal long before the record industry caught on.

MULTIPLE CHOICE

253. Which British band is often credited as one of the first to define the New Wave of British Heavy Metal (NWOBHM) with their 1980 debut album?

A) Saxon
B) Diamond Head
C) Iron Maiden
D) Angel Witch

254. The Welsh trio Budgie influenced later metal acts with early heavy riffs on songs like *Breadfan*. What year did they release their debut album?

A) 1969
B) 1971
C) 1973
D) 1975

255. Which Canadian band's 1983 album *Metal on Metal* helped establish the foundations of speed metal?

A) Anvil
B) Exciter
C) Razor
D) Voivod

256. The 1981 album *Welcome to Hell* by Venom is considered a major influence on which future metal subgenre?

A) Power Metal
B) Doom Metal
C) Black Metal
D) Glam Metal

257. The British group Diamond Head gained cult status for the song *Am I Evil?*, later covered by which major metal band?

A) Metallica
B) Megadeth
C) Anthrax
D) Slayer

258. Which German metal band broke into the international scene with their 1983 album Balls to the Wall?

A) Scorpions
B) Accept
C) Helloween
D) Grave Digger

TRUE / FALSE

259. Saxon's *Denim and Leather* became one of the defining albums of the NWOBHM era.

260. The underground U.K. label Neat Records was known for signing glam-metal acts from Los Angeles.

261. Exciter, one of Canada's earliest speed-metal bands, took their name from a Judas Priest song.

FILL-IN-THE-BLANK

262. The 1980 Judas Priest album *British _____* helped set the standard for classic heavy metal.

263. The underground British band Witchfynde helped popularize the occult-themed imagery common in the NWOBHM movement. Their debut album was *Give 'Em _____*.

264. The 1984 U.S. cult band Cirith _____ built a following among fantasy-metal fans with their album *King of the Dead*.

BEHIND THE TRACK.

"Metal on Metal" – Anvil (1982)

Recorded in Toronto on a limited budget, Metal on Metal captured the raw, unfiltered sound of early speed metal. Anvil's relentless touring and word-of-mouth reputation made the track an underground anthem in North America and Europe. Though mainstream commercial success never followed at the time, the album inspired future giants like Metallica and Slayer, who cited it as a blueprint for their early sound.

ROUND 23

SONGWRITING MASTERS & STUDIO WIZARDS

Behind every legendary performance was someone who knew how to shape it — a songwriter who could turn raw emotion into melody, or a producer who understood how to make a room full of instruments sound alive. These were the quiet architects of rock, balancing art and precision from the reel-to-reel days of the 1960s to the polished studio sound of the 1980s. Their influence is measured not just in hits, but in how their work changed the way records were made.

MULTIPLE CHOICE

265. Which producer is best known for his work with The Beatles, earning the nickname "The Fifth Beatle"?

A) Alan Parsons
B) Phil Spector
C) George Martin
D) Brian Epstein

266. The 1975 Fleetwood Mac album *Fleetwood Mac* marked the debut of which songwriting duo who reshaped the band's sound?

A) Danny Kirwan and Bob Welch
B) Christine McVie and John McVie
C) Peter Green and Jeremy Spencer
D) Lindsey Buckingham and Stevie Nicks

267. Jeff Lynne not only fronted Electric Light Orchestra but later became a sought-after producer. Which supergroup did he help form in 1988?

A) The Firm
B) Asia
C) Traveling Wilburys
D) GTR

268. Which songwriter wrote "Peaceful Easy Feeling" and later toured with the country-rock band Poco?

A) Timothy B. Schmit
B) Jack Tempchin
C) Bernie Leadon
D) Richie Furay

269. The song *Hotel California* was co-written by Don Felder, Don Henley, and which other member of the Eagles?

A) Glenn Frey
B) Joe Walsh
C) Randy Meisner
D) Bernie Leadon

270. Which British producer was behind landmark albums such as *The Dark Side of the Moon* (1973) and *Abbey Road* (1969), contributing engineering innovations like tape loops and layered effects?

A) Glyn Johns
B) Alan Parsons
C) Gus Dudgeon
D) Ken Scott

TRUE / FALSE

271. Todd Rundgren produced Meat Loaf's *Bat Out of Hell* but did not play any instruments on the album.

272. Phil Spector's "Wall of Sound" technique relied on overdubbing multiple instruments to create a dense, echoing effect.

273. Brian Eno produced the Talking Heads album *Remain in Light* and collaborated with David Bowie on his "Berlin Trilogy."

FILL-IN-THE-BLANK

274. Jeff Lynne of ELO produced the 1987 George Harrison single *Got My Mind _____ _____ _____*.

275. Producer Jimmy _____ worked with Tom Petty, Stevie Nicks, and The Heartbreakers, known for his polished yet natural production style.

276. The 1973 album *Goodbye Yellow Brick Road* was produced by Gus _____, who also worked extensively with Elton John during the 1970s.

DID YOU KNOW?

Many of rock's biggest hits were built in unexpected ways. When *Hotel California* was being written, Don Felder originally recorded the demo on a cheap cassette deck at home, adding layered guitar harmonies that Don Henley and Glenn Frey later shaped into lyrics about fame and excess. Jeff Lynne of ELO often wrote and arranged full songs in his head before entering the studio, dictating every part from memory. And producer Alan Parsons, while engineering *The Dark Side of the Moon*, experimented with tape loops of cash registers and coins to create the rhythm for "Money." The combination of inventive writing and fearless studio experimentation turned ordinary sessions into milestones of rock history.

ROUND 24

MYTHS, RUMORS & ROCK URBAN LEGENDS

Rock music has always carried its own folklore. Some stories began as late-night jokes, others as half-heard interviews or misread lyrics. A few were true, many were not, but all of them spread faster than press releases and lived longer than headlines. These myths became part of the culture, proof that the legends of rock were as unpredictable as the music itself.

MULTIPLE CHOICE

277. Which Beatles album fueled the "Paul is dead" rumor after fans analyzed its cover and lyrics for clues?

A) *Revolver*
B) *Abbey Road*
C) *Let It Be*
D) *Rubber Soul*

278. The long-standing rumor that a live shark was used in a shocking backstage incident has been linked for years to which rock band, though no credible evidence ever confirmed it?

A) Deep Purple
B) Aerosmith
C) Van Halen
D) Led Zeppelin

279. Which Fleetwood Mac song sparked gossip that Stevie Nicks used shawls and black clothing to signal an interest in witchcraft?

A) *Rhiannon*
B) *Gypsy*
C) *Dreams*
D) *Sara*

280. The urban legend that Led Zeppelin hid satanic messages in *Stairway to Heaven* by back-masking lyrics was publicly dismissed by which frontman?

A) Robert Plant
B) Jimmy Page
C) John Paul Jones
D) Ozzy Osbourne

281. Alice Cooper's shocking on-stage persona led to early-'70s tabloid stories claiming he had _____.

A) Bitten the head off a bat
B) Bitten the head off a chicken
C) Fainted mid-show
D) Used fake blood from ketchup packets

282. The long-running rumor that Gene Simmons of KISS had his tongue surgically altered for length has been proven to be _____.

A) True
B) False
C) Partially true
D) Undetermined

TRUE / FALSE

283. Keith Richards once claimed to have undergone a full blood transfusion to "cleanse" his system of drugs and later admitted to fabricating the claim.

284. Ozzy Osbourne's infamous bat-biting incident took place in 1982 during a concert in Des Moines, Iowa.

285. Jimmy Page of Led Zeppelin purchased a castle in Scotland that once belonged to novelist J.R.R. Tolkien.

FILL-IN-THE-BLANK

286. A long-standing rumor claimed that Phil Collins wrote the song _____ _____ _____ _____ about witnessing a man let someone drown, but the story has been proven false.

287. The myth that The Who destroyed their hotel rooms after every show began after _____ _____ accidentally drove a car into a hotel swimming pool in Flint, Michigan.

288. The long-running rumor, dubbed The Dark Side of the Rainbow, is that Pink Floyd synchronized *The Dark Side of the Moon* with the film The _____ _____ _____.

REMEMBER WHEN...

In October 1969, Detroit DJ Russ Gibb took a call on WKNR-FM, during which a listener suggested playing Beatles songs backwards to find clues that Paul McCartney was dead. Within days, college newspapers like The Michigan Daily printed "clue lists," and national outlets from Life to Time covered it. Capitol Records had to issue press statements denying McCartney's death — one of the first times a rock rumor made international news.

Enjoying these trivia questions?

We'd love to know what you think!

Leaving a quick review on Amazon helps other rock fans discover this book and keeps us inspired to create more. Just a few words about your experience makes a huge difference.

Scan the QR code to share your thoughts and keep the music alive.

SCAN ME

Scandal, Shock & Spectacle

By the late 1970s, rock had outgrown the clubs and taken over the headlines. The artists who once sang about rebellion were now being called into courtrooms and congressional hearings. Tour buses looked like rolling circuses, hotel managers prayed for quiet check-outs, and tabloids chased every broken guitar and police report.

Parents' groups warned that the music was corrupting youth. Politicians railed against lyrics they'd never actually heard. When MTV arrived, the spectacle went national — every outrageous tour, banned video, and late-night meltdown played out in living rooms across America. The PMRC hearings only added fuel, turning "Parental Advisory" stickers into badges of honor.

This was the era when outrage sold records and controversy filled arenas. If you remember when the evening news treated your record collection like evidence, you're in the right chapter.

ROUND 25

OUTRAGEOUS TOURS & BACKSTAGE STORIES

The concert road was as much about risk as it was about riffs. Broken contracts, chaotic sets, and tour-bus wars filled the margins of rock history. Here are incidents that made headlines and still raise eyebrows today.

MULTIPLE CHOICE

289. On November 20, 1973, at San Francisco's Cow Palace, which fan was pulled from the audience to complete a set after drummer Keith Moon passed out on stage?

A) John Furlong
B) Scot Halpin
C) Mike Danese
D) Tom Snyder

290. At the July 23, 1977, "Day on the Green" festival in Oakland, which band's security altercation with promoter Bill Graham's crew nearly ended their U.S. tour?

A) The Rolling Stones
B) Led Zeppelin
C) Aerosmith
D) Deep Purple

291. Which band's 1977–78 U.S. tour was dubbed the "Lace & Whiskey" tour, later known for backstage chaos that inspired their next album?

A) Alice Cooper
B) Mötley Crüe
C) Thin Lizzy
D) Uriah Heep

292. In 1982, Ozzy Osbourne was arrested after urinating on a monument near the Alamo while wearing his wife's dress. In which Texas city did this occur?

A) Dallas
B) Houston
C) San Antonio
D) Austin

293. The Rolling Stones' 1969 U.S. tour ended with a chaotic free concert at which venue, later depicted in the film *Gimme Shelter*?

A) Golden Gate Park
B) Altamont Speedway
C) Madison Square Garden
D) Shea Stadium

294. During their 1977 U.S. tour, Led Zeppelin's private Boeing 720 jet, nicknamed *The Starship*, became infamous for mid-air parties. Which artist later used the same plane for his own American tour?

A) Elton John
B) Peter Frampton
C) Alice Cooper
D) John Lennon

TRUE / FALSE

295. Aerosmith's 1977 show in Philadelphia was delayed when Steven Tyler was hit in the face by a thrown bottle.

296. On Van Halen's "1978 World Tour", the band's hotel destruction in Madison, WI, led to a lifetime ban from the Sheraton chain.

297. During Pink Floyd's 1977 "In the Flesh" tour, the final show in Montreal featured a notorious incident where Roger Waters spat at an aggressive fan. This moment provided the creative foundation for his next major project, the album "The Wall".

FILL-IN-THE-BLANK

298. Aerosmith's infamous "_____ Twins" nickname came from Steven Tyler and Joe Perry's excessive drug use and backstage volatility during the late 1970s.

299. In 1987, during Mötley Crüe's *Girls, Girls, Girls* tour, bassist _____ _____ collapsed from a heroin overdose — a near-death experience that later inspired their hit 'Kickstart My Heart.

300. During Alice Cooper's 1973 _____ _____ _____ tour, a gallows prop malfunctioned, nearly injuring the singer mid-show.

DID YOU KNOW?

Led Zeppelin's private Boeing 720, *The Starship*, wasn't just a plane. It was a flying hotel. Outfitted with a bar, bedroom, and electric organ, it became a headline symbol of 1970s rock excess. Crew members recalled mid-air parties between cities, complete with champagne service and poker games at 30,000 feet. The same jet was later leased by Elton John and Deep Purple and others, all eager to travel like Zeppelin had.

ROUND 26

BANNED OR CENSORED SONGS

Every era of rock had its rebels. Some songs pushed boundaries with their lyrics, politics, or sheer volume, making radio stations and record labels nervous. They were banned, censored, and protested, and the backlash only turned them into legends.

MULTIPLE CHOICE

301. The Kingsmen's 1963 hit *Louie Louie* was investigated by the FBI for what reason?

A) Alleged obscene lyrics
B) Communist messages
C) Copyright theft
D) Drug references

302. The Rolling Stones were forced to change the lyrics of *Let's Spend the Night Together* on which American TV program in 1967?

A) The Tonight Show
B) The Ed Sullivan Show
C) Shindig!
D) Hullabaloo

303. In 1969, *Je T'aime… Moi Non Plus* by Jane Birkin and Serge Gainsbourg was banned by the BBC for what reason?

A) Anti-religious content
B) Sexual explicitness
C) Political references
D) Drug advocacy

304. The song *Lola* by The Kinks was temporarily banned by the BBC because it mentioned which brand name?

A) Coca-Cola
B) Pepsi
C) Budweiser
D) Tang

305. Billy Joel's *Only the Good Die Young* was briefly pulled from U.S. radio in 1977 after complaints from which religious group?

A) Southern Baptists
B) Catholic organizations
C) Evangelical Lutherans
D) Seventh-day Adventists

306. *God Save the Queen* by the Sex Pistols was banned by the BBC and many retailers in 1977, yet reached what position in the U.K. Singles Chart?

A) #5
B) #3
C) #2
D) #1

TRUE / FALSE

307. The Doors' *Light My Fire* was cut short on *The Ed Sullivan Show* when Jim Morrison refused to alter the line "girl, we couldn't get much higher."

308. The Beatles' *A Day in the Life* was banned by the BBC in 1967 for alleged drug references.

309. In 1985 the song *Money for Nothing* by Dire Straits was banned worldwide for its depiction of materialism.

FILL-IN-THE-BLANK

310. The Who's *My Generation* was briefly banned by the BBC for fear that the lyrics might offend people with a _____ _____.

311. In 1971, radio stations refused to play John Lennon's *Working _____ _____* due to its lyrical profanity and anti-establishment message.

312. In 1970, radio programmers in several U.S. cities refused to play The Doors' _____ _____ because of its graphic lyrical references to blood on the streets.

DID YOU KNOW?

After Pink Floyd released *Another Brick in the Wall (Part II)*, South Africa's government banned the song outright. The apartheid regime feared the line *"We don't need no education"* would encourage student protests — and it did. What began as a rock lyric about rebellion in British classrooms became a rallying cry for freedom halfway around the world.

ROUND 27

ALBUM ART CONTROVERSIES

In rock's golden decades, album covers made statements. Some were artistic breakthroughs, others sparked outrage before the first note played. Retail bans, airbrushed reissues, and moral protests followed as designers pushed limits that record executives barely saw coming.

MULTIPLE CHOICE

313. The Beatles' 1966 "butcher cover" for *Yesterday and Today* featured the band in white coats with doll parts and raw meat. Why was it withdrawn?

A) It was considered disturbing and offensive to the public
B) It violated union photography rules
C) It depicted a parody of another band's album
D) It included hidden drug references

314. Jimi Hendrix's *Electric Ladyland* (1968) was initially sold in the U.K. with a controversial photo of:

A) A burning guitar
B) Nude women
C) A psychedelic collage of drugs
D) Political leaders

315. The Rolling Stones' *Sticky Fingers* (1971) cover, designed by Andy Warhol, featured:

A) A functioning zipper embedded over a jeans crotch
B) Real metal studs
C) Detachable fabric over a body
D) A lenticular photo

316. The Scorpions' 1976 album *Virgin Killer* was withdrawn and replaced due to its original cover depicting:

A) War imagery
B) A nude young girl
C) Religious symbols
D) Explicit lyrics printed on sleeve

317. The original cover of Guns N' Roses' *Appetite for Destruction* (1987) featured artist Robert Williams' painting of a robotic assailant being attacked by a metal avenger. Why was it replaced shortly after release?

A) Retailers refused to stock it due to sexual violence imagery
B) The band's label lost the rights to the artwork
C) MTV requested a redesign for broadcast promotion
D) A printing error forced a quick reissue

318. Which artist's 1979 album *Breakfast in America* drew complaints for its parody of the Statue of Liberty holding a glass of orange juice?

A) Supertramp
B) 10cc
C) Steely Dan
D) ELO

TRUE / FALSE

319. Black Sabbath's *Born Again* (1983) cover, showing a demonic baby, was banned in the U.K. for blasphemy.

320. The cover of Fleetwood Mac's *Rumours* (1977) was banned by several major U.S. retailers for being "too suggestive".

321. The original U.S. release of David Bowie's *Diamond Dogs* was airbrushed to remove the artist's canine genitals from the gatefold painting.

FILL-IN-THE-BLANK

322. The original cover of The Mamas and the Papas' *If You Can Believe Your Eyes and Ears* (1966) was altered to hide a visible _____ in the bathroom scene.

323. The original 1988 cover of Jane's Addiction's *Nothing's _____* sparked controversy for its depiction of nude women modeled after sculptures.

324. The 1985 album _____ by the Dead Kennedys led to a court case over the inclusion of H.R. Giger's poster *Landscape No. XX*.

REMEMBER WHEN...

There was a time when you bought a record and stared at the cover before you even dropped the needle. Sometimes the artwork said more than the music inside (or got the album pulled before it ever hit the racks)! Nobody needed social media to stir controversy; one bold photo, one printing mistake, or one offended parent could turn a record into a collector's legend.

ROUND 28

ROCK ARRESTS & LEGAL RUN-INS

Police raids, border checks, and courtroom appearances became part of the touring cycle for some of rock's biggest names. In those years, a mug shot could boost a reputation faster than a gold record. The same artists who filled arenas were often stopped at customs, booked in small-town jails, or hauled before judges eager to make an example of youth culture. It was a time when rebellion left paper trails, and the line between outlaw and entertainer blurred.

MULTIPLE CHOICE

325. In 1969, Jim Morrison was arrested during a concert in Miami on charges of:

A) Drug possession
B) Inciting a riot
C) Indecent exposure
D) Resisting arrest

326. Keith Richards' 1977 Toronto arrest for heroin possession led to what unusual sentence?

A) A $10,000 fine and one-year probation
B) A benefit concert for the blind
C) A lifetime ban from Canada
D) A suspended prison term

327. Paul McCartney spent ten days in a Tokyo jail in 1980 after customs agents found:

A) Hashish
B) Cocaine
C) LSD
D) Marijuana

328. By the late '70s, Fleetwood Mac's original guitarist Peter Green had slipped deep into isolation. His 1977 arrest came after he pulled a shotgun on whom?

A) A fan asking for an autograph
B) His accountant who tried to deliver a royalty check
C) A reporter chasing him for an interview
D) A promoter demanding he rejoin the band

329. In 1975, David Bowie was arrested in Rochester, New York, for possession of:

A) Heroin
B) Cocaine
C) Marijuana
D) Hash oil

330. Which Sex Pistols bassist was charged in connection with the 1978 death of Nancy Spungen?

A) Paul Cook
B) Steve Jones
C) Sid Vicious
D) Glen Matlock

TRUE / FALSE

331. In 1984, Mötley Crüe frontman Vince Neil was arrested for vehicular manslaughter and DUI after a crash that killed Hanoi Rocks drummer Nicholas "Razzle" Dingley.

332. Janis Joplin was fined in Tampa (1969) for "using indecent language" toward a police officer during a concert.

333. Ozzy Osbourne's 1982 arrest for biting a bat on stage resulted in a permanent ban from touring in the U.S.

FILL-IN-THE-BLANK

334. In 1970, Grateful Dead members Jerry Garcia and Bob Weir were arrested in _____ _____ for marijuana possession after a traffic stop.

335. In 1969, Keith Richards and Mick Jagger were sentenced to prison on drug charges but released on bail after public support led to the headline "Who Breaks a _____ on a Wheel?"

336. The Clash's Joe Strummer was arrested in 1980 for smashing his guitar over a fan's head during a concert in _____, _____.

DID YOU KNOW?

Two very different arrests helped shape later careers. In 1965, Frank Zappa was caught in a police sting at his Cucamonga studio for making a fake "stag-party" audio tape; he served 10 days in jail and later said the episode hardened his views on censorship. In 1975, Lemmy Kilmister was arrested in Toronto after customs confused his amphetamine sulfate with cocaine; the charge was dropped, but Hawkwind fired him, and within months he launched Motörhead.

ROUND 29

WILD MUSIC VIDEOS & MTV MOMENTS

By the mid-'80s, bands weren't just filming performances. They were staging mini-movies full of explosions, leather, and barely legal chaos. Some videos got banned, others won awards, and a few nearly burned down their own sets. Directors became as famous as the artists themselves, and one outrageous video could push a single up the charts overnight. What a time… Before the digital age sanitized everything!

MULTIPLE CHOICE

337. Which band's video for *"Hot for Teacher"* (1984) was nearly pulled from MTV for suggestive schoolroom imagery?

A) Mötley Crüe
B) Van Halen
C) Def Leppard
D) Twisted Sister

338. Which 1984 MTV experiment featured 18 different edits of the same rock video, aired in rotation to see which version viewers preferred?

A) Yes – "Leave It"
B) The Police – "Synchronicity II"
C) Van Halen – "Panama"
D) ZZ Top – "Sharp Dressed Man"

339. MTV initially refused to air *"Girls on Film"* (1981) by _____ because of nudity in its uncut version.

A) INXS
B) The Cars
C) Duran Duran
D) Roxy Music

340. Which hard-rock band made headlines when the pyrotechnics in their 1982 video shoot for *"Rock of Ages"* triggered a small stage fire?

A) Def Leppard
B) Judas Priest
C) Scorpions
D) AC/DC

341. The surreal 1980 short film for David Bowie's *"Ashes to Ashes"* cost over £250,000, making it one of the most expensive videos of its time. What technology drove its groundbreaking visuals?

A) Computerized frame-by-frame color manipulation
B) Quantel Paintbox (Early computer graphics)
C) Stop-motion puppetry
D) 3-D wire-frame animation

342. Which 1984 rock video was effectively blacklisted from MTV's U.S. rotation because it featured the band in drag?

A) Van Halen – "Hot for Teacher"
B) Twisted Sister – "We're Not Gonna Take It"
C) Queen – "I Want to Break Free"
D) Billy Idol – "Eyes Without a Face"

TRUE / FALSE

343. MTV's very first video broadcast in 1981 was *"Video Killed the Radio Star"* by The Buggles, featuring future Yes member Trevor Horn.

344. The Police's *"Every Breath You Take"* was filmed entirely in color to emphasize its romantic tone.

345. In 1987, MTV temporarily banned Mötley Crüe's *"Girls, Girls, Girls"* for featuring topless dancers filmed inside an actual strip club.

FILL-IN-THE-BLANK

346. Queen's groundbreaking 1975 video for *"Bohemian _____"* helped establish the modern music video format.

347. The Cars' 1984 hit _____ _____ _____ won MTV's first *Video of the Year* award for its pioneering use of computer-generated effects.

348. Peter Gabriel's "_____" (1986) combined stop-motion clay, puppetry, and pixelation to create a surreal visual masterpiece.

DID YOU KNOW?

When MTV Europe launched at 12:01 a.m. on August 1, 1987, the very first video it aired was Dire Straits' "Money for Nothing." The track's hook, "I want my MTV", was sung by Sting, whose publisher insisted on a songwriting credit because the melody echoed The Police's "Don't Stand So Close to Me." The irony ran deep… Mark Knopfler wrote the lyrics from the point of view of a blue-collar worker mocking rock-star excess and MTV itself. Yet that same video ended up launching the very channel it lampooned.

ROUND 30

THE PMRC ERA

By the time the cameras rolled in 1985, rock wasn't on trial for what it did, rather it was on trial for what it said. The Senate hearings turned Capitol Hill into a stage, complete with denim, hairspray, and defiance. Frank Zappa read from the Constitution, Dee Snider faced off against politicians in pearls, and even clean-cut artists like John Denver warned that censorship was just another form of book burning. What was meant to tame rock instead exposed just how out of touch its critics really were.

MULTIPLE CHOICE

349. Which 1985 Senate hearing became the centerpiece of the PMRC's campaign against explicit lyrics?

A) The National Music Standards Review
B) The "Filthy Fifteen" Hearings
C) The Parents Music Resource Center Hearings
D) The Senate Committee on Commerce, Science, and Transportation Hearings

350. Which Twisted Sister song was cited by the PMRC as promoting violence and rebellion?

A) "I Wanna Rock"
B) "We're Not Gonna Take It"
C) "Shoot 'Em Down"
D) "Burn in Hell"

351. During the 1985 Senate hearings, Frank Zappa warned that government labeling of music was like "treating dandruff by _____."

A) cutting your hair
B) censorship
C) decapitation
D) washing the brain

352. Which 1984 Prince song triggered Tipper Gore's outrage after her daughter heard its sexual lyrics?

A) "When Doves Cry"
B) "Darling Nikki"
C) "Erotic City"
D) "Head"

353. What did the PMRC's "Filthy Fifteen" list represent?

A) Songs banned from U.S. radio rotation
B) Fifteen tracks cited as the most explicit or offensive
C) The first albums labeled with warning stickers
D) Fifteen artists who refused to testify before Congress

354. Which heavy-metal band's album *Shout at the Devil* was accused of satanic influence during the PMRC hearings?

A) Judas Priest
B) Iron Maiden
C) Mötley Crüe
D) Slayer

TRUE / FALSE (3)

355. Dee Snider delivered his Senate testimony wearing a sleeveless denim vest and finished it off by flipping a table.

356. Ozzy Osbourne was personally summoned to testify at the 1985 PMRC hearings to defend his song *Suicide Solution.*

357. After the hearings, major labels voluntarily adopted the black-and-white "Parental Advisory: Explicit Lyrics" sticker to avoid government regulation.

FILL-IN-THE-BLANK (3)

358. The PMRC was co-founded in 1985 by Tipper Gore and other Washington wives known as the "_____ Wives."

359. Dee Snider's testimony directly challenged PMRC member _____ _____, calling her interpretation of Twisted Sister lyrics "a misunderstanding."

360. Frank Zappa released a 1986 single titled "_____ _____," mocking the group's crusade.

BEHIND THE TRACK.

Mötley Crüe's *"Bastard"* from *Shout at the Devil* landed on the PMRC's "Filthy Fifteen" list for "violence." The lyrics describe a brutal act of revenge — though Nikki Sixx later said it was an industry metaphor, not a murder scene. To the censors, it was proof that metal had gone too far; to fans, it was just another middle finger to authority. The controversy and resulting Parental Advisory sticker only helped the band's outlaw image.

The Legacy Lives On

By the late 1980s, rock had already proven it could outlast trends, critics, and the very technology that delivered it. The stage lights dimmed, but the sound never stopped. Those same songs kept echoing through car stereos, movie scenes, and reunion tours that felt more like family gatherings than concerts.

Records once sold in head shops turned into collectors' treasures. Vinyl made a comeback, and kids started spinning the same albums their parents wore out decades ago. Hollywood reached back for the soundtracks that defined a generation—AC/DC behind the chase scenes, The Rolling Stones over the end credits, Queen in the stadium mix.

Every few years, another band is inducted into the Rock & Roll Hall of Fame, and another crowd sings along to a song older than half the audience. What started in garages and nightclubs now fills arenas once again. The sound may be remastered, but the feeling is still the same.

ROUND 31

LIVE ALBUMS THAT MADE HISTORY

Some bands were born in the studio, but others only came alive under the lights. From Fillmore marathons to stadium thunder, rock's greatest live albums weren't just recordings; they were moments in time. These sets captured chaos, connection, and the roar of a generation. Some saved careers, others defined them, but all of them proved that rock's real magic happens onstage.

MULTIPLE CHOICE

361. Which 1976 double album is often credited with rescuing Peter Frampton's career and becoming one of the best-selling live albums ever?

A) *Wings Over America*
B) *Live and Dangerous*
C) *Frampton Comes Alive!*
D) *Alive!*

362. The Allman Brothers Band's *At Fillmore East* (1971) was recorded over how many nights at the legendary venue?

A) One
B) Four
C) Three
D) Two

363. Which band's 1970 live album *Get Yer Ya-Ya's Out!* captured performances from their American tour featuring Mick Taylor on guitar?

A) The Who
B) Led Zeppelin
C) The Rolling Stones
D) Faces

364. Cheap Trick's *At Budokan* (1978) became a U.S. hit only after success in which country?

A) United Kingdom
B) Japan
C) Germany
D) Australia

365. Which 1981 live album by Rush captured performances from the *Permanent Waves* and *Moving Pictures* tours?

A) *Exit... Stage Left*
B) *All the World's a Stage*
C) *Grace Under Pressure Tour*
D) *Show of Hands*

366. KISS's 1975 album *Alive!* became one of rock's most famous live records. Which producer was responsible for editing and mixing its final version?

A) Bob Ezrin
B) Eddie Kramer
C) Tom Werman
D) Jack Douglas

TRUE / FALSE

367. Lynyrd Skynyrd's *One More from the Road* (1976) was recorded live at the Fox Theatre in Atlanta, a venue the band helped save from demolition.

368. AC/DC's *If You Want Blood You've Got It* (1978) was the band's first live album recorded during the *Back in Black* tour.

369. Thin Lizzy's *Live and Dangerous* (1978) was recorded entirely live with no studio overdubs.

FILL-IN-THE-BLANK

370. *Made in Japan* (1972) captured Deep Purple's explosive *Machine Head* tour performances in the cities of Osaka and _____.

371. The 1979 album *Live Killers* documented the global rise of the British band _____.

372. Bruce Springsteen's *Live/_____–85* compiled recordings from a decade of legendary performances.

REMEMBER WHEN...

A live album was a test of whether a band could really play? You'd drop the needle and hear the amps hum, the crowd roar, and the frontman fighting to stay on pitch. No Auto-Tune, no safety net. Just raw rock caught in the wild, exactly the way it went down.

ROUND 32

ROCK IN FILM & POP CULTURE

Rock didn't fade when the curtain fell. It just found a bigger stage. From Easy Rider to Back to the Future, classic rock became Hollywood's favorite shorthand for rebellion, youth, and freedom. Whether roaring from car radios or blasting over final credits, these songs gave movies their pulse. Decades later, the same riffs still cue emotion, nostalgia, and goosebumps.

MULTIPLE CHOICE

373. Which 1969 film used Steppenwolf's "Born to Be Wild," turning it into an anthem for freedom and counterculture?

A) *Woodstock*
B) *Easy Rider*
C) *Midnight Cowboy*
D) *Vanishing Point*

374. Queen's "Bohemian Rhapsody" found new life in 1992 when featured in which hit comedy film?

A) *Bill & Ted's Excellent Adventure*
B) *Dazed and Confused*
C) *Wayne's World*
D) *The Wedding Singer*

375. AC/DC provided the soundtrack to which 1986 Stephen King-directed film?

A) *Maximum Overdrive*
B) *Firestarter*
C) *Christine*
D) *Silver Bullet*

376. Which Led Zeppelin song famously underscored the final scene of Cameron Crowe's *Almost Famous* (2000), symbolizing the band's lasting legacy?

A) "Kashmir"
B) "That's the Way"
C) "Tangerine"
D) "Stairway to Heaven"

377. The 1973 film *The Song Remains the Same* featured live performances and surreal sequences from which legendary rock band?

A) Pink Floyd
B) The Rolling Stones
C) The Who
D) Led Zeppelin

378. What 1985 blockbuster featured Huey Lewis and the News performing "The Power of Love," earning an Academy Award nomination?

A) *Ghostbusters*
B) *Top Gun*
C) *Back to the Future*
D) *Ferris Bueller's Day Off*

TRUE / FALSE

379. The Doors' music was excluded from the original 1979 release of *Apocalypse Now* due to rights disputes.

380. The Beatles' 1964 film *A Hard Day's Night* was named after one of John Lennon's early solo songs.

381. David Bowie's "Heroes" was used during the climactic tunnel scene of *The Perks of Being a Wallflower* (2012), introducing the song to a new generation.

FILL-IN-THE-BLANK

382. The 1982 teen comedy *Fast Times at Ridgemont High* opened with Jackson Browne's hit "_____ _____," setting the tone for the film's Southern California soundtrack.

383. *Dazed and Confused* (1993) opens with the rumbling of Aerosmith's _____ _____.

384. Pink Floyd's film adaptation of *The Wall* starred Bob _____ ,actor and frontman of The Boomtown Rats,as the rock star "Pink."

DID YOU KNOW?

When *Wayne's World* (1992) revived "Bohemian Rhapsody," Queen's surviving members were stunned. The song re-entered the Billboard Hot 100 nearly two decades after its debut, climbing to No. 2. Freddie Mercury had passed away just months earlier, but he'd already seen an early cut of the scene and loved it.

ROUND 33

ROCK & ROLL HALL OF FAME

Since 1986, the Rock & Roll Hall of Fame has been the scorecard for who truly shaped the sound. Some inductions made perfect sense, while others still spark arguments that never die. The first class set the bar and more than 350 names have followed. Not everyone agrees with the choices, but that's part of the fun.

MULTIPLE CHOICE

385. Which of these was **not** in the inaugural class of inductees in 1986?

A) Elvis Presley
B) The Beatles
C) Chuck Berry
D) Little Richard

386. What is the minimum number of years that must pass after an artist's first commercial recording before they become eligible for induction?

A) 10 years
B) 15 years
C) 20 years
D) 25 years

387. Which band was inducted into the Hall of Fame in 1997, the first year multiple major 1970s rock bands entered?

A) The Kinks
B) The Who
C) Crosby, Stills & Nash
D) Janis Joplin

388. The Hall of Fame defines categories for induction. Which of these is **not** one of the official categories listed on the Hall's site?

A) Performer
B) Early Influence
C) Technical Innovation
D) Non-Performer

389. Which group from the 1970s became the *first hard-rock band* inducted into the Rock & Roll Hall of Fame?

A) Led Zeppelin
B) Black Sabbath
C) Aerosmith
D) Deep Purple

390. Which 1970s punk band refused to attend their 2006 Rock & Roll Hall of Fame induction, sending a scathing handwritten note calling the Hall a "piss stain" and mocking the event instead?

A) The Clash
B) Ramones
C) Sex Pistols
D) Talking Heads

TRUE / FALSE

391. Lynyrd Skynyrd were inducted into the Rock & Roll Hall of Fame in 2006, nearly 30 years after the plane crash that claimed several members.

392. Multiple-inductee status means an artist has been inducted more than once—either with a band and solo career, or in separate groups.

393. The nominations for the Rock Hall are entirely fan-voted, and record sales determine the winners.

FILL-IN-THE-BLANK

394. When The Doors were inducted into the Rock & Roll Hall of Fame in 1993, Pearl Jam's _____ _____ performed with the surviving members in tribute.

395. Artists who worked behind the scenes such as producers, engineers, and executives are honoured under the "_____ _____ Award" category, named after the co-founder of the foundation.

396. When The Yardbirds were inducted into the Rock & Roll Hall of Fame, guitarist _____ _____ joked that he wasn't proud of the honor because the band had kicked him out.

BEHIND THE TRACK.

When the Rock & Roll Hall of Fame held its first induction ceremony in 1986, Chuck Berry kicked it off with "Johnny B. Goode," joined by Keith Richards on guitar. It was the perfect choice — the song that started it all, played by the man who wrote it, on the night rock & roll was officially recognized as history.

ROUND 34

SONGS STILL ON TOUR

Some songs never left the stage. They opened arenas in the '70s, ruled MTV in the '80s, and still close shows today. Different tours, same riffs... Real rock doesn't age out.

MULTIPLE CHOICE

397. Which 1970s arena band still closes nearly every concert with "Juke Box Hero"?

A) Foreigner
B) Boston
C) Kansas
D) Styx

398. Which British metal band still performs "Breaking the Law" and "Living After Midnight" on every tour?

A) Saxon
B) Iron Maiden
C) Judas Priest
D) Motörhead

399. Which 1980s hard-rock band continues to open shows with "Welcome to the Jungle" and close with "Paradise City"?

A) Poison

B) Motley Crüe
C) Guns N' Roses
D) Ratt

400. Which classic Who song has been the band's traditional concert closer since 1971?

A) "My Generation"
B) "Pinball Wizard"
C) "Baba O'Riley"
D) "Won't Get Fooled Again"

401. Which American band continues to feature "Barracuda" and "Crazy on You" in every setlist?

A) Pat Benatar & Neil Giraldo
B) Heart
C) Joan Jett & the Blackhearts
D) Scandal

402. Which Aerosmith song is not a permanent live staple?

A) "Walk This Way"
B) "Sweet Emotion"
C) "Dude (Looks Like a Lady)"
D) "Dream On"

TRUE / FALSE

403. Journey still ends nearly every concert with "Don't Stop Believin'," decades after its 1981 release.

404. REO Speedwagon rarely performs "Keep On Loving You" in concert today.

405. Cheap Trick still features "I Want You to Want Me" in every tour setlist, nearly 50 years after its release.

FILL-IN-THE-BLANK

406. The Rolling Stones have closed nearly every show since the late 1960s with "(_____ _____ _____ _____) _____," their signature encore.

407. Mötley Crüe still fires up arenas with their 1989 anthem "_____ _____ _____," often closing shows with pyrotechnics and smoke cannons.

408. Europe closes most of their festival sets with "The _____ _____," a song that has become one of rock's most iconic encores.

REMEMBER WHEN...

Remember when the encore lights came up and you already knew what was coming? "Free Bird," "Barracuda," "Juke Box Hero," "Won't Get Fooled Again." Decades later, the same riffs still shake the seats. These bands didn't retire their hits — they rebuilt their tours around them.

Concert-Going Nostalgia

Before online pre-sales and streaming encores, concerts were an adventure. You stood in line before sunrise, hoping the clerk still had good seats. You swapped bootleg cassettes that sounded like they'd been recorded from the parking lot. You wore a denim jacket covered in patches, stuffed a lighter in your pocket, and knew exactly when to flick it on.

The roar of the crowd was proof you were part of something real. You shouted every lyric until your voice was gone, felt the floor shake beneath your boots, and knew that what happened inside those walls could never be recreated. It was wild, imperfect, and absolutely unforgettable.

Now the lights are dimming, the band's heading back onstage, and this is your encore—the final round. These twenty fill-in-the-blank questions are for the die-hards who remember Ticketron lines, mail-traded tapes, and the magic of lighters glowing before cell phones took over the crowd.

Let's see how much of the show you still remember.

ROUND 35

YOU HAD TO BE THERE

FILL-IN-THE-BLANK

409. Before online ticketing, fans bought concert seats through _____, often waiting in line for hours outside record stores.

410. The outdoor New York festival that drew nearly 400,000 people in 1969 and helped inspire future rock gatherings was _____.

411. Bootleggers often recorded shows on portable _____ cassette recorders tucked under jackets.

412. The massive venue in Inglewood, California, known for hosting Led Zeppelin, Queen, and The Eagles was The _____.

413. Fans in the 1970s often held disposable _____ lighters in the air during power ballads before phones replaced them.

414. One of the most famous live albums of the 1970s, *Frampton Comes Alive!*, was recorded largely at San Francisco's _____ Ballroom.

415. Before official merch booths were common, fans bought homemade T-shirts and _____-_____ buttons outside arenas.

416. Before digital printing and official merch stands, fans covered their walls with fold-out concert _____ pulled from magazines or record sleeves.

417. Tape traders labeled their live recordings with the phrase "_____ _____ Only — Not for Sale" to avoid legal trouble.

117

418. The Grateful Dead's devoted followers who traveled show to show were called _____.

419. Many fans brought small handheld _____ cameras, hoping to capture blurry shots before security confiscated the film.

420. At late-'60s festivals, the air was thick with campfire smoke, incense, _____ oil, and a haze of marijuana drifting through the crowd.

421. When the first notes hit, fans rushed the front, gripping the cold metal _____ as if it were part of the show.

422. A popular 1970s slogan on bootleg shirts read "No Snow, No Show," a joking nod to Aerosmith's history with _____.

423. Before wristbands and digital tickets, fans guarded their prized proof of entry — a paper concert ticket _____ tucked in their jeans pocket all night.

424. Before tour apps and social media, fans learned the latest concert news from record-store bulletin boards, local newspapers and _____ _____.

425. Before arena doors opened, fans partied for hours outside — firing up grills, blasting tapes, and turning the _____ _____ into the first act of the night.

426. Many early light shows projected swirling colors onto screens using overhead _____.

427. Fans who followed entire tours by car or van were jokingly called road _____.

428. After a long encore, the arena lights came up to the crackle of the PA system and the faint smell of burning _____ from the stage pyrotechnics.

118

BONUS SECTION

Songs, Albums, & Scandals in Rock Music (1970s – 1980s)

ONE LAST ENCORE, BECAUSE THE SHOW ISN'T OVER YET!

ANAGRAM

Censored & Controversial Songs of the 1970s and 1980s

WORDS SCRAMBLED	CLUES	ANSWERS
HO TRYEPT MAWNO	MTV banned the video over its risqué bondage parody and gender-bending twist ending.	
AHHGYWI OT ELLH	Target of church-group protests and "satanic-panic" outrage, but not officially banned.	
ENO NI A OINLILM	Widely condemned for racist and homophobic lyrics. Some retailers/radio refused it.	
ISCDUEI NLIUOSOT	Faced controversy and lawsuit/press furor over alleged influence on suicide.	
YOBD AULNEGAG	MTV refused to air the video due to homoerotic imagery and near-nudity.	
HTO ROF AEHETCR	MTV/video controversy over sexual content.	
FTA TTOODBEM SIRGL	Longstanding lyric/content controversy.	
EXRLA	Banned by the BBC in 1984 for its explicit sexual lyrics; controversy helped propel it to No. 1 in the UK.	
SCTSASIPU UASSCUITTI	Banned by the BBC for being "offensive".	
DGO AVES HET QEUEN	Banned by the BBC for its direct attack on the British monarchy and institutions.	
EADD BAESBI	The song's narrative about child mortality and neglect was considered too dark for public consumption, even by the standards of early 1970s rock.	
LIAANM	Heavily censored for its explicit content and eventually omitted from the band's debut album (U.S. version).	

ANAGRAM

Shocking Albums of the 1970s and 1980s

WORDS SCRAMBLED	CLUES	ANSWERS
USHSEO FO HTE LOHY	Led Zeppelin's 1973 album with nude-children cover art that provoked bans.	
NIGRIV LRKELI	Scorpions' 1976 release with an infamous banned cover.	
TISKYC FGSIENR	Rolling Stones' 1971 LP with Andy Warhol zipper cover, censored by some retailers.	
SMEO RSGIL	Rolling Stones' 1978 album; lyrics baulked at and artwork stirred backlash due to band members in drag.	
UHTSO TA EHT VILDE	Motley Crue's 1983 album; accused of satanic influence.	
NUEBRM FO HTE ATESB	Iron Maiden's 1982 classic; boycotted by churches during satanic panic.	
ETTPEIPA ROF TECIDSTORUN	Guns N' Roses' 1987; original album cover banned for violent/sexual imagery.	
RNBO GAINA	Black Sabbath's 1983 LP with a disturbing "devil baby" cover.	
SCIATLP NOO BNDA	John Lennon's 1970 album; featured self-revelatory lyrics and themes, which included attacks on religious icons like Jesus and historical figures.	
AMAINL GNMAMITSE	Scorpions' 1980 album; cover of girl/dog sparked outrage.	
NI NCETRA	Scorpions' 1975 original album cover featured a visible breast that was censored in later releases.	
NIGER NI BODLO	Slayer's 1986 third studio album; controversial primarily due to the lyrical content of the opening track, "Angel of Death," which detailed the horrific human experimentation performed at the Auschwitz concentration camp.	

ANAGRAM

1970s and 1980s Rock Songs that Defied Authority

WORDS SCRAMBLED	CLUES	ANSWERS
RKBENGIA TEH LWA	Fist-pumping anthem of working-class frustration and rebellion against "the system."	
REW'E TON NONGA AKET TI	Bold rallying cry against authority figures and oppressive/unfair conditions.	
DSBE RAE BIGNNRU	Demand for justice and land rights; calling out government authority to "do the right thing."	
OIKB	Written as a tribute to South African anti-apartheid activist Steve Biko, who was murdered in police custody in 1977.	
ETH QEUEN SI DADE	Features anti-monarchist lyrics challenging Britain's most entrenched institution.	
GNIOG ERGDRUNDNUO	A chart-topping shot at political disillusionment and opting out of the establishment.	
TEH TNEO RSEFIL	Class-war snapshot; working-class protest versus elite privilege and power.	
I T'NWO CKAB NWOD	Partly inspired by the arson that destroyed Tom Petty's home; an anthem of resilience and standing firm in the face of adversity.	
ADB OPNTATEIRU	Industry-snubbing statement of independence meant to embrace being labeled "too crazy" or a "wild woman" by the music establishment for playing electric guitar and having a rebellious image.	
BOVNSIIUIDSS	Critique of conformity and social control; "be cool or be cast out."	
TEH UNGS FO XOITNBR	Street-level resistance to police and institutional pressure in Brixton.	
T'WNO GTE EOOLFD AIGAN	Anti-revolutionary song expressing disillusionment with political movements and power.	

MATCHING TRIVIA

Band ↔ Song/Album

1. LED ZEPPELIN   A. HOTEL CALIFORNIA

2. EAGLES   B. STAIRWAY TO HEAVEN

3. BLACK SABBATH   C. PARANOID

4. KISS   D. DARK SIDE OF THE MOON

5. DEEP PURPLE   E. DESTROYER

6. AEROSMITH   F. BLIZZARD OF OZZ

7. AC/DC   G. SMOKE ON THE WATER

8. BOSTON   H. RUN TO THE HILLS

9. OZZY   I. PUMP

10. LYNYRD SKYNYRD   J. GIRL'S GOT RHYTHM

11. PINK FLOYD   K. THIRD STAGE

12. IRON MAIDEN   L. FREE BIRD

MATCHING TRIVIA

Album ↔ Year

1. DARK SIDE OF THE MOON (PINK FLOYD)   A. 1973

2. BRITISH STEEL (JUDAS PRIEST)   B. 1983

3. NEBRASKA (BRUCE SPRINGSTEEN)   C. 1977

4. RUMOURS (FLEETWOOD MAC)   D. 1980

5. SOME GIRLS (THE ROLLING STONES)   E. 1975

6. PHYSICAL GRAFFITI (LED ZEPPLIN)   F. 1978

7. PYROMANIA (DEF LEPPARD)   G. 1981

8. MACHINE HEAD (DEEP PURPLE)   H. 1972

9. JAILBREAK (THIN LIZZY)   I. 1971

10. GHOST IN THE MACHINE (THE POLICE)   J. 1989

11. DISINTEGRATION (THE CURE)   K. 1976

12. WHO'S NEXT (THE WHO)   L. 1982

CROSSWORD

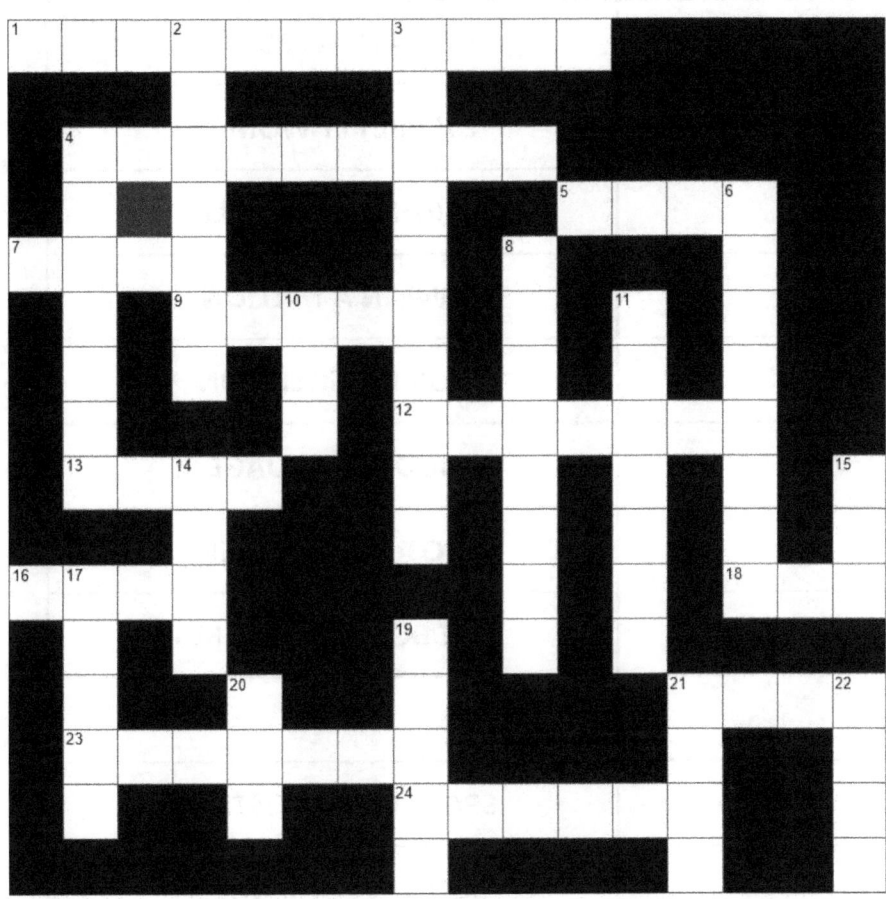

Across

1. "Breaking the Law" key song in the development of heavy metal.
4. The Who's explosive drummer; passed away in 1978.
5. Van Halen's synth-driven No. 1 smash (1984).
7. Prog supergroup with the 1982 hit "Heat of the Moment."
9. Derek & the Dominos' Clapton classic (1970).
12. Aerosmith's breakthrough ballad (1973, gained popularity in 1976).
13. Canadian prog trio; Neil Peart's precision powered their peak.
16. "Prince of Darkness," Sabbath singer turned solo star in 1980.
18. Powerhouse vocalist on Sabbath's Heaven and Hell (1980).
21. Fleetwood Mac's experimental double-LP 1979 follow-up.
23. The Police's 1978 single (written by Sting).
24. Los Angeles band behind "Hotel California".

Down

2. Pink Floyd's concept LP, inspired by George Orwell's book.
3. "Run to the Hills" defined early '80s metal.
4. Led Zeppelin's hypnotic centerpiece from their double album (1975).
6. Black Sabbath's 1970 metal anthem.
8. Lynyrd Skynyrd's extended guitar-hero epic (1973).
10. Prog greats behind "Roundabout".
11. Fleetwood Mac's 1977 drama-soaked blockbuster.
14. Chicago rockers best known for "Come Sail Away" (1977).
15. British hard rockers; Michael Schenker era defined the '70s peak.
17. U.S. hard-rock trio; self-titled debut landed in 1983.
19. "Bohemian Rhapsody" band fronted by Freddie Mercury.
20. Ozzy bit the head off a _____ on stage.
21. ZZ Top's 1975 Texas boogie staple.
22. Shock-rockers with makeup, pyro, and "Detroit Rock City."

ANSWER KEY

Censored & Controversial Songs of the 1970s and 1980s

WORD SCRAMBLE	ANSWERS
HO TRYEPT MAWNO	OH PRETTY WOMAN
AHHGYWI OT ELLH	HIGHWAY TO HELL
ENO NI A OINLILM	ONE IN A MILLION
ISCDUEI NLIUOSOT	SUICIDE SOLUTION
YOBD AULNEGAG	BODY LANGUAGE
HTO ROF AEHETCR	HOT FOR TEACHER
FTA TTOODBEM SIRGL	FAT BOTTOMED GIRLS
EXRLA	RELAX
SCTSASIPU UASSCUITTI	SPASTICUS AUTISTICUS
DGO AVES HET QEUEN	GOD SAVE THE QUEEN
EADD BAESBI	DEAD BABIES
LIAANM	ANIMAL

ANSWER KEY

Shocking Albums of the 1970s and 1980s

WORD SCRAMBLE	ANSWERS
USHSEO FO HTE LOHY	HOUSES OF THE HOLY
NIGRIV LRKELI	VIRGIN KILLER
TISKYC FGSIENR	STICKY FINGERS
SMEO RSGIL	SOME GIRLS
UHTSO TA EHT VILDE	SHOUT AT THE DEVIL
NUEBRM FO HTE ATESB	NUMBER OF THE BEAST
ETTPEIPA ROF TECIDSTORUN	APPETITE FOR DESTRUCTION
RNBO GAINA	BORN AGAIN
SCIATLP NOO BNDA	PLASTIC ONO BAND
AMAINL GNMAMITSE	ANIMAL MAGNETISM
NI NCETRA	IN TRANCE
NIGER NI BODLO	REIGN IN BLOOD

ANSWER KEY

1970s and 1980s Rock Songs that Defied Authority

WORD SCRAMBLE	ANSWERS
RKBENGIA TEH LWA	BREAKING THE LAW
REW'E TON NONGA AKET TI	WE'RE NOT GONNA TAKE IT
DSBE RAE BIGNNRU	BEDS ARE BURNING
OIKB	BIKO
ETH QEUEN SI DADE	THE QUEEN IS DEAD
GNIOG ERGDRUNDNUO	GOING UNDERGROUND
TEH TNEO RSEFIL	THE ETON RIFLES
I T'NWO CKAB NWOD	I WON'T BACK DOWN
ADB OPNTATEIRU	BAD REPUTATION
BOVNSIIUIDSS	SUBDIVISIONS
TEH UNGS FO XOITNBR	THE GUNS OF BRIXTON
T'WNO GTE EOOLFD AIGAN	WON'T GET FOOLED AGAIN

ANSWER KEY

Band ↔ Song/Album

1. LED ZEPPELIN → (B)
2. EAGLES → (A)
3. BLACK SABBATH → (C)
4. KISS → (E)
5. DEEP PURPLE → (G)
6. AEROSMITH → (I)
7. AC/DC → (J)
8. BOSTON → (K)
9. OZZY → (F)
10. LYNYRD SKYNYRD → (L)
11. PINK FLOYD → (D)
12. IRON MAIDEN → (H)

Album ↔ Year

1. DARK SIDE OF THE MOON (PINK FLOYD) → (A)
2. BRITISH STEEL (JUDAS PRIEST) → (D)
3. NEBRASKA (BRUCE SPRINGSTEEN) → (L)
4. RUMOURS (FLEETWOOD MAC) → (C)
5. SOME GIRLS (THE ROLLING STONES) → (F)
6. PHYSICAL GRAFFITI (LED ZEPPLIN) → (E)
7. PYROMANIA (DEF LEPPARD) → (B)
8. MACHINE HEAD (DEEP PURPLE) → (H)
9. JAILBREAK (THIN LIZZY) → (K)
10. GHOST IN THE MACHINE (THE POLICE) → (G)
11. DISINTEGRATION (THE CURE) → (J)
12. WHO'S NEXT (THE WHO) → (I)

CROSSWORD

A favor before you go...

If you enjoyed this trivia book, we'd be grateful if you shared your thoughts in a quick Amazon review.

Your feedback not only helps other fans discover similar books, it keeps projects like this alive at Backstage Classics. Every review fuels new books, videos, and ways to celebrate the music we all love.

Scan the QR code to leave your review and keep the community rocking.

SCAN ME

KEEP THE NEEDLE MOVING

If you want more stories, more context, and deeper dives into the bans, boycotts, sleeve swaps, and court fights you met here, come find us on **Backstage Classics** on **YouTube**.

That's where we share:

- Rare concert footage and iconic live performances from the '60s, '70s, and '80s
- Deep-dive documentaries and stories behind the music, bands, and albums that defined rock
- Classic rock, hard rock, blues rock, arena anthems, and more — all in one place

Search **Backstage Classics (YouTube)** and hit **Subscribe**. Drop a comment with the question that stumped you or the one you nailed because you were there. If a story in this book jogged a memory (first show, first "banned" single, first long drive with FM blasting), share it.

That's how this history stays alive.

See you backstage!

ANSWER KEY

ROUND 1: U.S. Garage & Surf Pioneers

1. A
2. A
3. B
4. C
5. A
6. C
7. True
8. True
9. False – it was released in 1965.
10. Spring/Fender
11. Dirty Water
12. Dale

ROUND 2: The British Invasion

13. D
14. A
15. D
16. B
17. B
18. A
19. True
20. True
21. False – he was 20 years old when the song was recorded in 1965.
22. string

23. razor blade
24. Keith Richards

ROUND 3: Psychedelia & The Summer of Love

25. B
26. C
27. A
28. C
29. B
30. B
31. True
32. False – the lead sound was a 12-string Rickenbacker guitar, not a sitar.
33. True
34. McKenzie
35. San Francisco
36. Hollywood

ROUND 4: Breakthrough Albums of the Late '60s

37. C
38. B
39. A
40. A
41. B
42. B
43. True
44. True
45. False – The album was recorded in both Los Angeles and New York
46. Abbey
47. Boys

48. Beggars
49. B
50. C
51. A
52. B
53. B
54. D
55. True
56. True
57. False – Their set was infamously tainted by numerous technical issues
58. acid
59. Star Spangled Banner
60. Peace
61. C
62. A
63. B
64. B
65. D
66. C
67. True
68. False – the group toured Scandinavia in 1968 before the album's release using the name *The New Yardbirds*.
69. True
70. Morning
71. Jimi Hendrix
72. Paranoid
73. C
74. C
75. B
76. B

77. C
78. D
79. True
80. True
81. True
82. Teenage Wasteland
83. Money
84. artist

ROUND 8: 1960s Rock Milestones Quiz (Decade Review)

85. D
86. C
87. B
88. C
89. B
90. D
91. True
92. False – it was assembled from sessions across several studios over many months.
93. True
94. White
95. Poor Boys
96. rock

ROUND 9: Arena Rock Anthems & Sing-Along Choruses

97. C
98. B
99. A
100. B

101. D
102. C
103. True
104. True
105. True
106. Livgren
107. We Will Rock You
108. Scholz

ROUND 10: Classic Rock Radio Kings

109. B
110. B
111. D
112. D
113. A
114. B
115. False – it was a dedication after his passing, but the song was written earlier.
116. True
117. True
118. Lindsey Buckingham
119. Airliner
120. Szymczyk

ROUND 11: Power Ballads & Big Hooks

121. B
122. C
123. C
124. A

125. A
126. A
127. True
128. False – it was widely aired and helped launch the band internationally.
129. True
130. Of The Tiger
131. When Wet
132. 1988

ROUND 12: U.S. vs. British Rock Rivalries

133. C
134. C
135. A
136. D
137. D
138. A
139. True
140. False – Bad Company was the supergroup that included Paul Rodgers and Simon Kirke from Free, Mick Ralphs from Mott the Hoople, and Boz Burrell from King Crimson.
141. False – *Hysteria* by Def Leppard eventually outsold it worldwide, though *Hi Infidelity* led early in the decade.
142. Orchestral Rock (aka Symphonic Rock)
143. Steve
144. Back in Town

ROUND 13: MTV Rock Breakouts

145. D
146. A
147. A

148. B
149. B
150. A
151. True
152. False – MTV began to expand its playlist to include pop, R&B, and new wave, but rock remained central to the channel's lineup throughout the decade.
153. True
154. Black and White
155. 1984
156. Van Halen

ROUND 14: Guitar Heroes & Solo Legends

157. B
158. D
159. B
160. C
161. A
162. B
163. False – he is most associated with the Gibson SG.
164. True
165. False – Vai was a student of Satriani before both became world-famous solo guitarists.
166. Frankenstrat, Frankenstein or Frankie
167. Alien
168. Blizzard of Ozz

ROUND 15: Frontmen Who Ruled the Stage

169. A
170. B
171. C

172. C
173. A
174. B
175. True
176. True
177. True
178. in the Night
179. Gramm
180. Thunder and Lightning

ROUND 16: Women Who Rocked the Airwaves

181. D
182. A
183. C
184. A
185. B
186. C
187. True
188. True
189. False – Blondie was formed as a full group from the start, co-founded with guitarist Chris Stein.
190. Smyth
191. Vocal Performance
192. Donna

ROUND 17: Lost Bands of the '70s

193. C
194. A
195. A

196. A
197. D
198. B
199. True
200. False – they released two albums on the label, *Detective* (1977) and *It Takes One to Know One* (1978).
201. True
202. Relf
203. Dog
204. Lloyd-Langton

ROUND 18: One-Album Wonders

205. C
206. A
207. D
208. B
209. D
210. A
211. True
212. False – they issued only one, *Women and Children First* (1970).
213. True
214. progressive
215. Hoyle
216. Summer

ROUND 19: Underrated Guitar Gods

217. C
218. B
219. B

220. A
221. C
222. A
223. True
224. False – he is best known for his use of Fender Stratocasters.
225. True
226. Street Crawler
227. Walkways
228. Wonder

ROUND 20: Overlooked Prog & Art-Rock Heroes

229. B
230. A
231. C
232. B
233. B
234. A
235. True
236. False – *The Snow Goose* is famous for being a largely instrumental concept album; the band removed all lyrical vocals before release due to a legal dispute with the novella's author, Paul Gallico.
237. True
238. Harvest
239. Forneria Marconi
240. instrumental/symphonic

ROUND 21: Remembering FM Favorites

241. B
242. B
243. A

244. C
245. B
246. A
247. False – *"Baby Come Back"* hit No. 1 for Player in early 1978.
248. True
249. False – it was released in 1976 and became their biggest hit.
250. Thomas
251. Balin
252. Paul Pena

ROUND 22: Cult Metal & Underground Scenes

253. C
254. B
255. A
256. C
257. A
258. B
259. True
260. False – Neat Records focused on British heavy-metal bands like Raven and Venom.
261. True
262. Steel
263. Hell
264. Ungol

ROUND 23: Songwriting Masters & Studio Wizards

265. C
266. D
267. C

268. B
269. A
270. B
271. False – Rundgren played guitar and arranged several tracks during the sessions.
272. True
273. True
274. Set On You
275. Iovine
276. Dudgeon

ROUND 24: Myths, Rumors & Rock Urban Legends

277. B
278. D
279. A
280. A
281. B
282. B
283. True
284. True
285. False – Page bought Boleskine House near Loch Ness, which had belonged to occultist Aleister Crowley, not Tolkien.
286. In The Air Tonight
287. Keith Moon
288. Wizard of Oz

ROUND 25: Outrageous Tours & Backstage Stories

289. B
290. B

291. A
292. C
293. B
294. A
295. False – Steven Tyler was injured by a cherry bomb thrown on stage
296. True
297. True
298. Toxic
299. Nikki Sixx
300. Billion Dollar Babies

ROUND 26: Banned or Censored Songs

301. A
302. B
303. B
304. A
305. B
306. C
307. True
308. True
309. False – It was only temporarily restricted in Canada in 2011 for a homophobic slur.
310. speech impediment or stutter
311. Class Hero
312. Peace Frog

ROUND 27: Album Art Controversies

313. A
314. B

315. A
316. B
317. A
318. A
319. False – it drew criticism but was never officially banned.
320. False – The album cover was never banned; however, it sparked controversy due to the two wooden balls visible between Mick Fleetwood's legs. These were parts of a lavatory chain he wore as a good-luck charm, ironically contributing to the image becoming one of the most recognizable of the decade.
321. True
322. toilet
323. *Shocking*
324. *Frankenchrist*

ROUND 28: Rock Arrests & Legal Run-Ins

325. C
326. B
327. D
328. B
329. C
330. C
331. True
332. True
333. False – He was treated for rabies. However, he was not arrested and continued touring within weeks.
334. New Orleans
335. Butterfly
336. Hamburg, Germany

ROUND 29: Wild Music Videos & MTV Moments

337. B
338. A
339. C
340. A
341. B
342. C
343. True
344. False – It was shot in moody black-and-white by director Godley & Creme to underscore its darker themes.
345. True
346. Rhapsody
347. You Might Think
348. Sledgehammer

ROUND 30: The PMRC Era

349. D
350. B
351. C
352. B
353. B
354. C
355. False – He famously spoke extemporaneously, calm and articulate, defying senators' expectations of a "wild rocker."
356. False – Ozzy Osbourne was never called to testify at the 1985 PMRC hearings. Though his song *"Suicide Solution"* drew fire from parent groups, his legal battles over it came later — in courtrooms, not on Capitol Hill.
357. True
358. Washington

359. Tipper Gore

360. Porn Wars

ROUND 31: Live Albums That Made History

361. C

362. D

363. C

364. B

365. A

366. B

367. True

368. False – It was recorded during the *Powerage* tour in 1978, two years before *Back in Black*.

369. False – Although recorded at concerts in London, Toronto, and Philadelphia during 1976–77, much of the album was later polished in the studio under producer Tony Visconti. Phil Lynott insisted the energy was real, but the perfection was a little studio-assisted.

370. Tokyo

371. Queen

372. 1975

ROUND 32: Rock in Film & Pop Culture

373. B

374. C

375. A

376. C

377. D

378. C

379. False – *The End* by The Doors opens the film and remains one of its defining sequences.

380. False – The title came from an offhand remark by Ringo Starr after a long recording session. Lennon then wrote the song *after* the title was chosen for the film. John Lennon's solo work began in 1970.
381. True
382. Somebody's Baby
383. Sweet Emotion
384. Geldof

ROUND 33: Rock & Roll Hall of Fame

385. B
386. D
387. C
388. C
389. A
390. C
391. True
392. True
393. False – The Rock & Roll Hall of Fame isn't fan-voted, and record sales don't decide the winners. A committee selects the nominees, over 1,000 industry experts vote, and the fan ballot counts as just one vote. Inductees are chosen for influence and impact, not sales.
394. Eddie Vedder
395. Ahmet Ertegun
396. Jeff Beck

ROUND 34: Songs Still on Tour

397. A
398. C
399. C

400. D
401. B
402. D
403. True
404. False – It remains one of their most-performed live songs and a guaranteed crowd favorite.
405. True
406. (I Can't Get No) Satisfaction
407. Kickstart My Heart
408. Final Countdown

ROUND 35: You Had to Be There

Fill-in-the-Blank

409. Ticketron
410. Woodstock
411. Sony
412. Forum
413. Bic
414. Winterland
415. pin-back
416. posters
417. For Trade
418. Deadheads
419. 35 mm or Instamatic
420. patchouli.
421. barricade or guardrail
422. cocaine
423. stub
424. radio stations

425. parking lot

426. projectors

427. hogs, warriors or rats

428. gunpowder

SOURCES AND REFERENCES

The following books, magazines, archives, interviews, liner notes, and official materials were consulted to verify dates, releases, and historical details.

Ambrose, Joe. *Gimme Danger: The Story of Iggy Pop.* Omnibus Press, 2009.

American Film Institute Catalog. *Easy Rider* (1969). Columbia Pictures — verified soundtrack listing including Steppenwolf's "Born to Be Wild."

Associated Press Wire Reports (Sept. 1985) — summaries of testimony by Zappa, Snider, and Denver.

Atlantic Records. *Who Made Who* (AC/DC), 1986 — official soundtrack credits for Stephen King's *Maximum Overdrive.*

BBC Archives — *Deep Purple: Made in Japan Revisited* (documentary transcript, 2018).

BBC News Archives — "Banned Covers: The Stories Behind Rock's Most Controversial Art" (documentary transcript, 2015).

BBC News Archives — *Rock and the Law* (documentary transcript, 2018).

BBC News Archive (August 1, 1987) — report on the launch of MTV Europe.

BBC Program Review Board Minutes (1965–1971).

BBC Radio 1 — *Friday Rock Show* archives.

BBC Radio 1 archives — *Sounds of the Seventies* sessions.

BBC Radio Archives — *The Story of The Animals* (documentary transcript, 2000).

BBC Radio 4 — *The Producers* (documentary series, 2004–2006).

BBC Radio 4 — *The Beatles' Abbey Road and the Paul is Dead Myth* (2019).

Beaumont, Mark. *The Story of Britpop.* Ebury Press, 2023.

Beck, Jeff. *Blow by Blow* liner notes, Epic Records (1975).

Bethel, Tom. *The Making of the Allman Brothers' Fillmore East Recordings.* Capricorn Records Archive Notes, 1971.

Bethel Woods Center for the Arts — archival history on the Woodstock site and schedule.

Billboard — "Judas Priest Celebrate 50 Years of Heavy Metal with New Tour" (March 2022).

Billboard — "Aerosmith Announce 'Peace Out' Farewell Tour — See the Full Setlist" (September 2023).

Billboard — "Mötley Crüe's 'Kickstart My Heart' Still Rules the Arena" (2022).

Billboard — "REO Speedwagon Still Rocking After 40 Years on the Road" (2021).

Billboard — *Tour Files* (1972–1985).

Billboard archives (1973–1988) — album credits and chart data.

Billboard Magazine archives — "Hot 100 Number Ones: 1980–1988."

Billboard Magazine Archives (1970–1985) — chart performance and release data for major live albums including *Frampton Comes Alive!*, *At Fillmore East*, *Alive!*, and *At Budokan*.

Billboard Magazine Archives (1983–1986) — articles on MTV programming, video premieres, and censorship.

Billboard Magazine Archives (Sept.–Oct. 1985) — coverage of PMRC hearings, Dee Snider's remarks, and reactions from musicians and senators.

Billboard Magazine Archive — "Censorship and Radio Standards" (1978).

Billboard Magazine archives, 1970–1989.

Billboard — "MTV and the 1980s Rock Boom."

Billboard — "Rolling Stone Archives: Classic Rock Radio and the Rise of FM Power" *(entry retained as originally provided)*.

Billboard — "MTV Programming Experiments." April 14, 1984 — coverage of Yes's "Leave It" video versions.

Bogdanov, Vladimir, et al. *All Music Guide to Rock.* Backbeat Books, 2002.

Buckley, David. *Strange Fascination: David Bowie – The Definitive Story.* Virgin Books, 2000.

Cheap Trick — official discography: *At Budokan* production details and release chronology.

Classic Albums: *Frampton Comes Alive!* Documentary. Eagle Rock Entertainment, 2013.

Classic Albums: *Hysteria* (documentary). Eagle Rock Entertainment, 2002.

Classic Rock Magazine — "Arena Rock and the Sound of the 70s."

Classic Rock Magazine — "When Video Changed the Sound of Rock."

Classic Rock Magazine — "The Rise of the Power Ballad."

Classic Rock Magazine — "Women Who Broke the Sound Barrier."

Classic Rock Magazine — "The Lost Bands of the 1970s."

Classic Rock Magazine — "The Cult of the One-Album Wonder."

Classic Rock Magazine — "When Album Art Crossed the Line." Future Publishing, 2013.

Classic Rock Magazine — "Queen Conquers South America" (2020).

Classic Rock Magazine — "Keith Richards and the Toronto Trial" (2015).

Columbia Records — Woodstock release schedules and Santana discography notes (1969).

Coppola, Francis Ford. *Notes on the Making of Apocalypse Now.* Zoetrope Studios, 1979 — licensing details for The Doors' "The End."

Crüe, Nikki Sixx. Interview in *Hit Parader*, Jan. 1986 — explanation of "Bastard" as a metaphorical lyric.

Crowe, Cameron. Interview, *Rolling Stone*, Sept. 2000 — *Almost Famous* and touring with The Allman Brothers Band.

Davis, Stephen. *Hammer of the Gods.* William Morrow, 1985.

Def Leppard — Official Website: production notes on "Rock of Ages" video shoot.

Deram/Arista — official label and album notes for Renaissance *(as provided)*.

Discogs.com and IMDb (Music Video sections) — cross-verification of release years and director credits.

DreamWorks / Paramount Pictures. *Almost Famous* (2000) — soundtrack and commentary; "Tangerine" usage verified by Cameron Crowe.

Eder, Bruce. "Blue Cheer Biography." In *AllMusic Guide to Rock.* Backbeat Books, 2002.

Egan, Sean. *The Rolling Stones and Philosophy* (discography essays on late-'60s albums). Open Court, 2008.

Everett, Walter. *The Beatles as Musicians Vol. 1.* Oxford University Press, 2001.

Fender — historical records *(as provided)*.

Fletcher, Tony. *Moon: The Life and Death of a Rock Legend.* HarperCollins, 1999.

Florida Board of Executive Clemency — "Jim Morrison Pardon," 2010.

Future Rock Legends (futurerocklegends.com) — cross-reference of inductee years, multiple-inductee records, and Rock Hall categories.

Geffen Records. *Dazed and Confused: Original Motion Picture Soundtrack* (1993) — Aerosmith's "Sweet Emotion" opening track listing.

Gilliland, John. *The Pop Chronicles: The Story of Rock 'n' Roll* (1969 radio documentary transcripts, University of North Texas Archives).

Gilliland, John. *The Pop Chronicles: The Story of Rock 'n' Roll* (University of North Texas Archives).

Gilmore, Mikal. *Stories Done: Writings on the 1960s and Its Discontents.* Free Press, 2008.

Gore, Tipper. *Raising PG Kids in an X-Rated Society.* Abingdon Press, 1987 — PMRC founders' perspective and rationale.

Guitar Player Magazine — interviews (1974–1988).

Guitar World Magazine Archives (1975–1992).

Halford, Rob. Interview in *Kerrang!* No. 98 (1985) — Judas Priest's reaction to the Filthy Fifteen.

Hjort, Christopher. *Strange Brew: Eric Clapton and the British Blues Boom 1965–1970.* Jawbone Press, 2007.

Hoskyns, Barney. *Across the Great Divide: The Band and America.* Hyperion, 1993.

Hoskyns, Barney. *Hotel California: The True Life Adventures of Crosby, Stills, Nash, Young, and The Eagles.* Wiley, 2006.

Joel, Billy. *The Stranger* 30th Anniversary Edition commentary. Columbia Records.

Kansas — *40th Anniversary Documentary.* Sony Legacy, 2016.

Kerrang! archives (1980–1985).

Lang, Michael, with Holly George-Warren. *The Road to Woodstock.* Ecco, 2009.

Lewis, Dave. *Led Zeppelin: A Celebration.* Omnibus Press, 1991.

Lewis, Dave. *Led Zeppelin: The Concert File.* Omnibus Press, 1997.

Lewisohn, Mark. *The Complete Beatles Recording Sessions.* Hamlyn, 1988.

Los Angeles County Superior Court — *People v. Dead Kennedys* (1986).

Mallet, David (director). Interview on "Ashes to Ashes" production. *Blender*, July 2002.

Makower, Joel. *Woodstock: The Oral History.* Doubleday, 1989.

Marsh, Dave (ed.). *The Rolling Stone Illustrated History of Rock and Roll.* Random House, 1992.

Marsh, Dave. *The Heart of Rock & Soul: The 1001 Greatest Singles Ever Made.* Plume, 1989.

Marks, Craig, & Tannenbaum, Rob. *I Want My MTV: The Uncensored Story of the Music Video Revolution.* Dutton, 2011.

May, Brian. Interview, *Mojo Magazine*, April 2002 — confirmation that Freddie Mercury previewed the *Wayne's World* sequence before his death.

McParland, Robert. *The Rock Music Imagination.* Lexington Books, 2017.

Metal Hammer — retrospectives on NWOBHM.

Miles, Barry. *Pink Floyd: The Early Years.* Omnibus Press, 2006.

Mitchell, Rick. *Rock Chronicles: The 100 Greatest Albums of the 1970s.*

Morse, Steve. *Boston: The Authorized Biography.* HarperCollins, 2006.

MTV Archives — "The Launch of MTV: August 1, 1981."

MTV History — "The Transatlantic Rivalry That Built the 1980s."

Neat Records, Attic Records, Roadrunner Records — official label histories.

Official artist discographies and liner notes (Journey, Foreigner, Def Leppard, Heart, Scorpions).

OfficialKISSOnline.com — archival notes on recording and overdub locations for *Alive!* (Cobo Hall, 1975).

Osbourne, Ozzy. Interview in *Circus Magazine*, Dec. 1985 — clarification that "Suicide Solution" addressed alcohol abuse.

PFM — coverage as provided under Record Collector/official discographies *(entry retained within combined label/source items)*.

Popoff, Martin. *Black Sabbath: Doom Let Loose.* ECW Press, 2006.

Popoff, Martin. *The Deep Purple Family: Every Album, Every Song.* Wymer Publishing, 2018.

Priore, Domenic. *Pop Surf Culture: Music, Design, Film, and Fashion from the Bohemian Surf Boom.* Santa Monica Press, 2008.

Queen — official archives: *News of the World* tour notes (1977–1978).

Queen Online (official site) — background on "I Want to Break Free" video controversy.

Record Collector Magazine (U.K.) — reissue features, 1990–2020.

Repertoire Records and Esoteric Reissues archives (2000–2020).

RIAA — Gold & Platinum Database (1979–1988 certification records; artist-specific entries cited in text).

RIAA Historical Notes — "Parental Advisory Label History." Recording Industry Association of America (riaa.com) — documentation of the sticker's voluntary adoption in 1985.

Ritchie Yorke. *The History of Rock 'n' Roll: The Definitive Story and Documentary.* Doubleday, 1986.

Rolling Stone — "The 100 Greatest Guitarists of All Time."

Rolling Stone — "The 25 Biggest Urban Legends in Rock History" (2017).

Rolling Stone — coverage of the 1986 inaugural Rock Hall ceremony and subsequent inductions.

Rolling Stone — "Foreigner Extend Farewell Tour as 'Juke Box Hero' Keeps Packing Arenas." August 2023.

Rolling Stone — "Guns N' Roses: The Songs They Never Drop from the Setlist." Future Publishing, July 2023. *(publisher line mirrors original entry)*

Rolling Stone — "Heart Bring Back the Thunder with 'Barracuda' and 'Crazy on You.'" June 2022.

Rolling Stone — "Journey Keep the Faith (and the Hits) Alive with 'Don't Stop Believin.'" May 2023.

Rolling Stone — "The Rolling Stones' Enduring Tradition: Every Show Ends with 'Satisfaction.'" 2022.

Rolling Stone Archives — contemporary and retrospective reviews of *Live at Leeds*, *Made in Japan*, *One More from the Road*, and *Exit... Stage Left*.

Rolling Stone Archives — artist interviews and video-production features (1981–1987).

Rolling Stone, January 1993 — report on The Doors' induction and Eddie Vedder's guest performance.

Rosen, Craig (ed.) *(implicit in Billboard archival references; retained as originally provided)*.

Rush.com (official band site) — tour and recording data for *Exit... Stage Left* (1980–81).

Seger, Bob. *Night Moves* liner notes and Capitol Records documentation.

Selvin, Joel. *Summer of Love: The Inside Story of LSD, Rock & Roll, Free Love, and Revolution in the 1960s.* Cooper Square Press, 1994.

Setlist.fm Archives — verified tour setlists for Foreigner, Judas Priest, Guns N' Roses, The Who, Heart, Aerosmith, Journey, REO Speedwagon, Cheap Trick, The Rolling Stones, Mötley Crüe, and Europe (accessed 2023).

Shadwick, Keith. *Jimi Hendrix: Musician.* Backbeat Books, 2003.

Shapiro, Harry. *Jimi Hendrix: Electric Gypsy.* St. Martin's Press, 1990.

Sinclair, Paul. *Queen: As It Began.* Smith Gryphon, 1992.

Sound on Sound Magazine — "Inside the Studio with Joe Walsh and Bill Szymczyk."

Spitz, Bob. *Barefoot in Babylon: The Creation of the Woodstock Music Festival, 1969.* W. Morrow, 1979.

Sony Legacy — *Kansas 40th Anniversary Documentary* (2016).

Summit Entertainment. *The Perks of Being a Wallflower* (2012) — soundtrack credits including David Bowie's "Heroes."

The New York Times — "Psychedelic Music Arrives," March 1966.

The Times (London), June 29, 1967.

Thompson, Dave. *Smoke on the Water: The Deep Purple Story.* ECW Press, 2004.

Thomson, Dave. *The Kinks: All Day and All of the Night.* Backbeat Books, 2002.

U.S. Department of Justice — District Court Records, *People v. Led Zeppelin Security Team* (Oakland, CA, 1977).

U.S. Federal Bureau of Investigation — "The Louie Louie Investigation" (declassified report, 1964–65).

U.S. Senate Committee on Commerce, Science, and Transportation — Record Label Warning Hearings. *Congressional Record*, Sept. 1985.

U.S. Senate Committee on Commerce, Science and Transportation — Hearing on "Record Labeling," September 19, 1985 — official transcript, U.S. Government Printing Office.

Unterberger, Richie. *Turn! Turn! Turn!: The '60s Folk-Rock Revolution.* Backbeat Books, 2002.

Unterberger, Richie. *Eight Miles High: Folk-Rock's Flight from Haight-Ashbury to Woodstock.* Backbeat Books, 2003.

Unterberger, Richie. *Urban Spacemen and Wayfaring Strangers: Overlooked Innovators and Eccentric Visionaries of '60s Rock.* Hal Leonard, 2000.

Variety (March 2006) — confirmation of Lynyrd Skynyrd's 2006 Rock Hall induction class following the 1977 plane crash.

Variety Magazine — "Inside the Soundtrack Revolution: *Saturday Night Fever*," Dec. 1977 — origin of Bee Gees substitution for rock-based early drafts.

Vaughan, Stevie Ray. *Texas Flood* studio session documentation (1983).

Visconti, Tony. Interview in *Sound on Sound*, August 2007 — commentary on studio overdubs for Thin Lizzy's *Live and Dangerous*.

Waksman, Steve. *This Ain't the Summer of Love: Conflict and Crossover in Heavy Metal and Punk.* University of California Press, 2009.

Warner Bros. Records. *The Song Remains the Same* (1976) — Led Zeppelin live film and soundtrack documentation.

Welch, Chris. *Deep Purple: The Illustrated Biography.* Omnibus Press, 1982.

Welch, Chris. *Led Zeppelin: Dazed and Confused – The Stories Behind Every Song.* Thunder's Mouth Press, 2002.

Welch, Chris. *Pink Floyd: The Stories Behind Every Song.* Thunder's Mouth Press, 2002.

Whitburn, Joel. *Rock Tracks: 1955–1991.* Record Research, 1992.

Whitburn, Joel. *Top Pop Singles 1955–1999.* Billboard Books, 1999.

Whitburn, Joel. *Top Pop Singles 1955–2001.* Record Research, 2001.

Whitburn, Joel. *Top Pop Albums 1955–2001.* Record Research, 2001.

Wikipedia contributors — "Woodstock," "MTV," "Arena Rock," and related entries (accessed 2024).

Wladleigh, Michael (director). *Woodstock* (1970 film) — official soundtrack album documentation.

Woodstock (1970 film) — dir. Michael Wadleigh; official soundtrack album documentation. *(retained as provided)*

Zappa, Frank. *The Real Frank Zappa Book.* Poseidon Press, 1989 — includes direct quotes and commentary from Senate testimony.